The View from the Drain

The View from the Drain

PORTER PENN

LUMINARE PRESS

WWW.LUMINAREPRESS.COM

Printed in the United States of America

Cover Design by Nina Leis

Luminare Press
442 Charnelton St.
Eugene, OR 97401
www.luminarepress.com

LCCN: 2020905022
ISBN: 978-1-64388-342-7

To my daughters, Jamie and Lisa,
and to my granddaughters, Kylie and Emery.
The genesis of this collection of reminiscences and
observations came from my desire for them to know me—
not as Mom or Gram, but as a unique individual
with hopes, dreams, "firsts", and who learned
many lessons throughout life's journey. I hope they
learn much about me from this collection.

To my friend and mentor, Robert Bush,
an author himself of four inspirational books.
I can't thank him enough for his support,
guidance, and friendship.

To Nancy Myers, who would have been so proud
to have seen this book come to fruition.

To my friends and to the readers whom I don't yet know.
It is my hope that the stories in this collection will
resonate in a way that is unique to you.

And, finally, to Vivianne,
who inspired me to keep writing.

Contents

Saving Porter

I almost drown in a Wisconsin lake when I was four. I was just learning the fundamentals of staying afloat when my Aunt JoAnn, a mediocre swimmer, scooped me up and carried me out to the deeper water. One float too far and she was beyond where her feet could touch the bottom. The weight of a four-year-old proved to be too much for her and caused us to sink. I remember her clutching me hard as we both, gasping for breath, struggled to get back to the surface.

After what felt like an eternity, my mother finally noticed the struggle and dove in, fully clothed, to save us. To this day, I am as sure as I was at the age of four, she was more intent on saving her sister than on saving me.

I quickly learned that if you want to be saved, you have to learn to save yourself.

By the age of six, I was an excellent swimmer.

The View from the Drain

L ately, I have been writing about my past, experiences I've had and lessons I've learned. Today, I am writing about today, a subject I have avoided since I became the S-word.

I've never minded birthdays, enjoyed the celebration, and proudly announced my age. After all, through the veiled mask of self-deception, I have looked and acted exactly as I did in my 30's—the pinnacle of my womanhood and physical endurance. Why should I mind birthdays? When I turned 60, I joked with my kids that I was circling the drain, not because I felt that way, but because the age itself frightened me. Still, through that veiled mask of self-deception, to myself, I looked and acted the same as I always had.

This year, I became the S-word. No longer circling the drain, I was in the Drain. For the first time, I didn't want to tell anyone my age. In the eyes of society, I was an old woman. My friends said, "You look really good for your age. I didn't realize you were THAT old." Well, then, thanks for that.

Today, after I showered, dressed, curled my hair, and put on makeup, I looked in the mirror. Front view—I looked good. Almost 30. Then, I had the bad judgement to look at my profile. The veiled mask of self-deception dropped.

What I saw was a woman, however thin, with a slight turkey neck and an osteopenia spine. I looked at the front view again. Nope, I wasn't 30. The mask was off.

As a child, I was fascinated with old people. I wondered what they thought about. They were so different, they scared me. I never wanted to be one of "them". Still, I wondered what it was like to be them. Surely, it must be awful.

When I was six, I used to play in the neighborhood with Donny, Denny, and Delbert Reed. Their father was a podiatrist. We called him Doc. His name was Walter Reed. Dr. Walter Reed. His wife, Lois, was a full-time housewife. I thought Lois was an old person. She wore flowered dresses to clean the house in and signature black shoes. They had a chunky one-and-a-half-inch heel and tie laces that went up to her ankle. Turtleneck shoes! Black turtleneck shoes! She wore them every day and for every occasion.

Now, keep this in mind. I was six, and to a child that young, everyone over the age of 12 is old. Lois was probably in her late 30's when I played with her boys, but to me, she was really, really old.

I began to get the notion that when I got old, it was a requirement that I wore those chunky, ugly, turtleneck shoes. I am not sure why I came to that conclusion. My mother didn't wear shoes like that and neither did any of the other moms in the neighborhood. But Lois was really old to me, and she became, in my six-year-old mind, the poster child for old age. I never wanted to get old—EVER.

In fact, I was so troubled by this notion that one evening when I was sitting on my dad's lap, reading the red-bound book of fairy tales, I suddenly blurted out, "I am never getting old!!" My dad laughed and said, "Well, you don't have to worry about that for a long, long time. But, why don't you want to get old?" Almost in tears, I said, "If I get old, I will have to wear Lois Reed shoes, and I don't want to!" My dad tried to convince me that Lois's choice of shoes was a personal matter, and that I would never be required to wear shoes like that.

He was wrong. I just knew it.

Now that I am in the Drain and have reached septuagenarian status, the view from here is considerably different from what I had imagined. Dad was right, it turns out. There is no shoe requirement. I continue to wear stilettos, sling-backs, and Converse All Stars as the occasion dictates. None of them are black.

When you are in the Drain, you still have so many choices. You can look up toward the light or look the other way, which is a scary proposition. For the record, for years I have been trying to find a way to get out of death. I'm still working on it. When I have it figured out, I will let you know.

So, I have chosen to look up at the light. The view from here is amazing. Every experience now has infinite impact and indelible memories. Food tastes better, love is deeper, family more cherished, and passion is white hot. And, yes, sorrow is deeper and despair magnified. Ever the teacher, every day offers me the opportunity to share my accumulated wisdom, my lifetime journey, and those special memories that have defined me. I love that about my life.

As for how I look, I still hope to look good. Someone recently said, "If only our eyes saw souls instead of bodies, how very different our ideals of beauty would be". I have learned that beauty on the outside is fueled by the glow inside. It is that glow that makes one attractive and beautiful, despite one's age. I hope that I can continue to project that glow.

The View from the Drain is what life should always have been about. Being in the moment, savoring the moment, and sharing memories in the making, not tearing through the moment to get to the next thing. I am glad I am getting to enjoy and share this view.

And the best part is, there is no shoe requirement.

Dad

From the age of three until about seven, I sat on my Dad's lap every night while he read me stories. He was tall and thin, strong and gentle. I loved the warmth of him and the safety of his lap. A toolmaker and a skilled woodworker, I could smell the scent of cut wood as he held me close to him. We owned a set of brightly bound books, each with unique stories of history, geography, nursery rhymes and fables. My favorite was the red-bound book of fables and nursery rhymes. I would stare at the intricate illustrations as my Dad read with his cigarette-softened voice. Most nights, I would eventually close my eyes and drift away to the sound of him. I could feel him close the book, gently pick me up and carry me to my bed. I could feel him kiss me softly on the cheek and pull the covers up around me. I was safe.

My dad grew up in the 1920's in Benton, Illinois, population 800. A town on the border of Kentucky, it had all the charm of the Deep South, Southern accents included, and all of the deep prejudice of the South in the 1920's.

My Dad's prejudice was deep and strong, aimed not only at black people, but people of different religions and countries. I inherited many things from my Dad, his creativity and his love of reading among them, but prejudice was not one of them. Black people were referred to using the N-word, spear-chuckers, and jigaboos. Catholics were mackerel snappers; Jews were Kikes: Italians were WOPS and Guinea grease-balls. At four and five, I didn't understand these words. What I did understand was the change in him when he said them. His face hardened, his voice raised, and his body stiffened in a way to which I was unaccustomed. This was not the dad of the red book and the soft voice.

At age six, my world began to slowly change. My Dad was a skilled toolmaker who sold power tools to companies in states to which I had never been. He wore a suit and smelled like cologne when he travelled. He thought of my brother and me when he was on the road, which was often, and he never failed to bring us something fun. There were toys and trinkets, t-shirts and hats. Nothing elaborate. On one return trip from Ohio, he brought me a glass snow globe with a penguin inside. I loved the way the snow softly fell on the penguin's head when I shook the globe. It was quiet, peaceful, and soft.

It was after that trip that the arguing began. My Dad wanted to move to Cincinnati. My mother refused to leave her eight brothers and sisters, who were, by all accounts, more important to her than we were as a family. They were in, and Dad was out. Out of that job, and soon, out of our lives emotionally.

Dad took a job as a tool and die maker on the 3 PM to 11:00 PM shift. Gone was the suit and wonderful smelling cologne and gone were the nights of the red book and the safety of his lap.

He wore coveralls, smelled like grease and steel, and had a new smell—the smell of alcohol. When I did see him, which was no longer often, it was when I was awakened late at night to the sound of yelling and the breaking of beer bottles in the sink. I would wander sleepily down the stairs in search of comfort, and, as had become the norm, there was none. My Dad couldn't even comfort himself, so there was no comfort to give to me. My mother had no desire to comfort a child she cared so little for. Go back to bed was the directive, and so I would. Soon, I no longer wandered downstairs when I was awakened. I stayed in bed and pretended I heard nothing.

On the weekends and at times when he was working a day shift, my Dad would drive my brother and me to places we wanted to go. Sometimes he drove us both together; most times it was separately. We both knew that he shouldn't be driving and that he drove "funny". We dreaded these trips, every time, mostly because we knew that each trip was punctuated with a stop at his favorite bar. He would tell us that he was going to "stop off" and that it would only be a couple of minutes. In actuality, it was an hour or more. If my brother and I were together, it was awful, but tolerable. We did the silly things brothers and sisters do to pass the time sitting in a car alone together.

The times I was all alone were different. I wiggled, was fearful of strange cars that pulled in to the parking lot, and worried that he would forget about me altogether. Who could I tell? Could I go inside the bar? Sometimes I would think of my snow globe with the penguin inside. I thought of how softly the snow fell on the penguin's head, and I felt peaceful and safe.

I am not sure exactly when it happened, but my Dad was no longer my Dad, but my father. I was distancing myself from something that was leaving me. In a child's desperate reach for survival, I clung to the only person who could take care of me—my mother. She was a woman fraught with hysteria and anger and had very little regard for me. Still, that was all I had.

I drank the Kool-Aid, so to speak. I did everything she asked, regardless of whether or not it made sense. Over and over, I tried to convince her that I was a good person and an obedient daughter. It was, it seems, never good enough. I did distance myself from my father, and, as an obedient daughter, blamed him for all of the problems in our family.

My Dad was smart and sensitive and creative. I know that now. Aside from his raging prejudice, he was, at heart, a good man. But as a teenager, when he reached out to talk to me of his work and of his life, I shut him down and turned my back on him.

Many years later, after I gave birth to my daughter Lisa, he tried—though limited—to be a caring grandfather to her. I saw the soft side of him and thought of the red book and the safety of his lap. And I was angry. Angry for lost time and angry for lost love.

Many lifetime miles have changed me. I no longer carry the anger I once did. By the time I reached an age of understanding and could talk to him, he had died.

Though I will never know for sure, I believe my Dad had a life outside our family that he longed for. I think he spent the majority of his adult lifetime missing that. I never asked him that, but I surely would now. But I know this—I remember the red book and the softness of his voice, and I miss him.

Understanding sometimes takes a lifetime to come. I'm glad it came for me. I wish I could have told him.

Todd

I had my first kiss when I was five. My best friend and kindergarten partner, Todd, lived four houses down from me on Southgate Avenue. Every day, he and his two older sisters would join me on our walk to Jefferson Elementary School. We would walk slowly by the neighborhood houses until we reached the forest preserve. Most days, Todd and I would lag behind to talk, while his sisters took the lead. We had to cross a bridge that spanned Thorn Creek, a deep and rapidly flowing creek that ebbed and flowed with the seasons. Always, we had to be wary of loose boards on the bridge that were broken from weather or vandalism. It wasn't scary, back then, walking through the woods. Our greatest fear was navigating the missing boards or watching the rising creek level during the spring snowmelt and constant rains.

Todd and I were in different kindergarten classes, but had recess together. We were playground soulmates. We pushed each other on the swings, played kickball, and played King of the Hill. A huge mound of dirt left from playground renovation was a gift to all of us looking for a challenge and an adventure during our 30 minutes of outside freedom. Whoever scaled to the top of the hill first was the victor. Not many girls played King of the Hill. It was physical, exhausting, and hard to play in a dress. But

I had Todd, who always protected and looked out for me.

One day after school, it was just Todd and me walking home through the woods and across the bridge. His sisters had afternoon activities that kept them behind that day. We talked of playground fun and the woods around us.

When we reached the sidewalk leading to his house, we both lingered. Suddenly, he leaned forward and gave me a peck on the lips, the childhood equivalent of passion. The second his impulse passed, he said, "Don't you tell your mother," and ran full speed into his house. Ahh, such is the passion of a five-year old.

There never was a second kiss, though we remained playground soulmates throughout elementary school. I think of Todd, our neighborhood, and our playground adventures often.

We all need a Todd in the phases of our lives, to keep us happy, protected and safe, and inspired to try things we might not otherwise try.

While the neighborhood that was once tranquil and idyllic is now riddled with bullets and gang graffiti, my memory of that moment is just as I experienced it. Places, too, experience change, just as we each do—some for the better, some for the worse. But the memory of a moment in time is ours, impervious to change.

Rose

I was told that I was a musical prodigy. I had no idea what that meant when I was nine. All I knew, from my Aunt Betty who was a symphony cellist and a professional piano teacher, was that I was a mediocre piano player. My mother thought it would "look good" if I had some musical education and asked her if she would teach me to play the piano.

We had an upright piano in our house. I remember going with my mother to purchase it from a man who had too little space and too little desire to have a piano. It wasn't just any piano—it was a player piano. It had special paper-like rolls that you could insert inside, causing it to play itself. I loved that piano and loved how it played! We purchased it in 1955 for $20.

Alas, that piano did not like me. I struggled to synchronize my left and right hand to create the music. I have always been a one-task, one-function-at-a time kind of girl, and so, coordinating different left-and right-hand functions was a challenge. That piano repeatedly told me that it could play itself and certainly didn't need me pounding on it in some futile attempt to create music.

During one piano lesson, while I was struggling for coordination, my Aunt Betty looked at me closely and said, "You know, there is a better instrument for you. You have big hands and long fingers, and I think the bassoon would be just right for you." Indeed, it was. Called "The Clown of the Orchestra", it was a tall, hulking thing that very few would want to play. From an aesthetic point of view, I didn't want to, either. I much preferred the flute or French horn, something more delicate. Still, there was something about it. We were like two awkward souls finding our way.

I affectionately called her Rose because of her rosewood color. When I first learned to play her, she was taller than me by 12 inches. I trained and studied, and before long, I became quite proficient. So much so that as a 4th grader, the junior high school band director wanted me to play with their band and orchestra. Three times a week, my mother would drive Rose and me to the junior high for practice. I was excused from my 4th grade afternoon classes and was totally overwhelmed by these "older" musicians, though musically I could more than hold my own.

By the time I was 12, I auditioned for the Chicago Heights Symphony Orchestra's Youth Opportunity Contest. The winner would be a guest soloist at a performance with the symphony. There were many, many applicants, and I, frankly, just auditioned on a whim.

Rose and I had a spiritual connection. When I blew my breath into her, she responded with a tone and timbre that was magnificent. Rose was my savior and my escape. She took me from a world of anger and dysfunction to a world of beauty, symphony, and the brilliance of classical composers. I felt safe and whole and accomplished in that world. For once, I was more than good enough.

When I received a letter in the mail telling me that I had won the opportunity contest for the youth division and that I was being invited to be the guest soloist with the symphony, I remember my mother saying, "Oh God, what do we do now? I didn't think you would actually win!" Her fear, of course, was that I might embarrass her, as I apparently had frequently done in other aspects of my life.

Rose and I knew what to do. We memorized Mozart's Concerto in B Flat for bassoon and practiced up to 4 hours a day for seven weeks in preparation.

The actual performance was frightening for a 12-year-old. The audience was packed; the professional musicians, while kind and gentle, were intimidating. Music critics from the newspaper were in the audience. I remember taking a deep breath and saying, "Here we go, Rose. We can do this!" With that, Rose and I walked across the stage, bowed to the audience, and gave what was, as always for us, a flawless performance. The audience and music critics agreed. That was the first time I was called a child musical prodigy.

Rose and I had countless adventures together. We attended an eight-week music camp for gifted children, spent six weeks in Europe playing concerts in five different countries, played concerts with the Chicago Youth Symphony at Orchestra Hall, Chicago's equivalent of Carnegie Hall. We won a full music scholarship to Illinois Wesleyan University.

By the end of my college freshman year, I was conflicted. Living away from my home of anger and dysfunction, my need to escape to a world of musical magnificence lessened. The academics of orchestra, band, quintets, and musical theory were tedious. Part of the academics required me to play other instruments for which I had neither the affinity nor the desire. I felt like I was cheating on Rose.

A crushing breakup with a fellow musician sealed the deal. I was done with being a musician. Being around him was too painful. I needed to move on.

When I went back home for the summer, I talked to my Dad. Though alcohol sedated most of the time, he still retained his gentle nature and level head. He said, "Whatever you choose to do, I know you will make the right choice, and you'll be successful." Breaking the news to my mother was quite another experience. Hysterical and judgmental, she yelled, "What are you going to do now? What are you going to do? You were good at that, good at music. What else will you do??" In my mother's estimation, I was generally a worthless person who just happened to have musical talent, which along the way, brought some positive attention to her. Though IQ tested at 134, she thought that I was incapable of doing anything besides making music. What to do, indeed.

In the fall, I returned to college as a sophomore studying English and Psychology. Rose was packed away and put on the shelf.

I miss my adventures with Rose. She filled a desperate need for escape at a time when I needed it most. I'm sure she misses me, too. I blew life into her and she responded with magical, melodious music. She will always be one of the best parts of me. But, as I have learned, not the only part.

The Neighborhood

I grew up in a blue collar, working class neighborhood in a suburb south of Chicago. The houses were small, brick bungalows, the streets unpaved. Twice a year, the city maintenance crew came through to spread oil on the streets to keep the road dust down. I always disliked those days because, if I rode my bike too soon after they were done (which I seemed to do every time), my bike was covered with oil and so was I.

The neighborhood was, for want of a better word, cozy. The neighbors were all, in different degrees, friends, except for a few who were reclusive and a few who were somewhat odd. Once a month, the neighborhood women played canasta at a designated house. I loved when canasta club was held at our house! My mother made a marshmallow, whipped cream fruit salad, and there were tons of mixed nuts to snack on, things we rarely had at our house. The down side was that there were no children allowed at canasta club. My brother and I were confined to our rooms.

I loved my room. Though small, it was completely paneled with beautiful knotty pine boards. My grandfather and my Dad, both skilled woodworkers, converted the attic of our small home in to a two-bedroom living space. Purchasing the best grade knotty pine wood, their conversion project lasted more than three months. I loved the smell of freshly sawed wood as they were working!

The finished product was beautiful. The rooms had built-in dressers, inset bookcases, beautiful ceiling fans, and decorative inlaid wood designs on the walls. At night, lying on my bed, with only a reading lamp lit, I would stare at the knots in the pine, conjuring up faces and pictures in the wood. My room was almost perfect.

Almost perfect except for one thing. I had no door. No closeable door that every child needs for privacy. There was a beautifully trimmed doorway, but no door. My parent's bedroom was ten feet away from mine, and it, too, had no door.

From the time I was ten until I was seventeen, the only thing I ever asked for as a birthday or Christmas present was a door for my room. When I went to college and moved into my first apartment, my room at home still had no door. Maybe they thought if I didn't have a door, I couldn't slam it when I was angry (which was often, except for when I was making music).

We had street vendors in our neighborhood. At least two times a week, they would come with their trucks or peddlers' bikes, hawking their wares. John was the scissor grinder. He had a grinding wheel attached to the front of his peddlers' bike and sharpened scissors, knives, and any yard tool that needed sharpening.

But my favorite street peddler was George. He was an Italian-American who, though he spoke fluent English, retained a very heavy Italian accent. Twice a week, he would drive his truck up the block to sell fresh fruit, vegetables, and, in the winter, mittens and gloves that his wife had knit. We could hear him long before we ever saw his truck. He would slowly drive and lean out the driver's side window chanting, "Apple-a, Apple-a, Peach-aye".

We would run out of the house to see what he was

selling that day because it varied from visit to visit and from season to season. We all loved George. He was a tall man with a dark, black mustache, a flat cap always on his head, and a smile that lit up the neighborhood. I especially remember his hands, long fingered and gentle as he put our purchased produce into brown bags.

I wore his wife's knitted mittens when I went sledding down "the hill" in the winter. "The hill" was a vacant lot at the end of our block that had a wonderful, drastically sloping hill beside it. At the first sign of measurable snowfall, all of the neighborhood kids would spontaneously congregate to go sledding. We were careful not to sled so fast that we slid into the major street at the bottom of the hill. But sometimes we forgot.

We were an athletic bunch, us neighborhood kids. Girls and boys alike, we were in the middle of everything. There were softball games weekly in a large yard at the end of the block, explorations in the alley behind our houses that yielded unexpected treasures, fishing in Thorn Creek that ran behind our neighborhood, and forest preserve adventures where we jumped from high branches in the giant apple tree and ate so many apples, we all had belly aches. In the winter, we ice skated at the neighborhood park where they flooded the tennis courts with water and let it freeze. It made a spectacular skating rink.

In every group, there are people who lead, people who follow, and people who carry their burdens like an overstuffed backpack.

Judy Rabideau had an overstuffed backpack. When Judy was seven, her parents left her to watch her four-year-old sister while they went grocery shopping. In the forty-five minutes they were gone, a lit candle fell on her sister, igniting her clothes and the sofa. With unusual presence of mind for a seven-year-old, she dragged her sister, Tonette, engulfed in flames, into the bathroom, lifted her into the bathtub, and immersed her in water. Tonette's face was saved from the flames, but not much else.

Judy carried the heavy backpack of her guilt for years after the incident. The weight of it made her angry and hostile and entitled to take her frustration out on those of us who were gentler, and yes, weaker.

For months I was the target of her aggression. I think she gravitated towards me among the neighborhood kids because I was an easy target, and she could release her aggression multiple times a day, lessening her own pain.

After months of witnessing this, my Dad, at that time still engaged in our family, sat me down for a talk. He said, "You don't have to take that from Judy or anyone. You need to stand up for yourself. You need to be stronger. She targets you because she sees you as weak." I knew my mother felt that way about me, but I didn't know that my Dad saw me as weak, too. But his intentions were different. He wanted to save me from pain, not inflict it.

I thought about that talk for weeks. I didn't know what it meant to be strong, and I continued to be the unwilling target of her hostility.

One summer afternoon, a number of us neighborhood kids were playing in my backyard. Judy, of course, was there, hurling her insults with staggering precision. I thought over and over, as she assaulted me, about my Dad's advice to be strong.

At the side of the yard was my broken child's chair that my Dad was going to repair. The leg that had fallen off was lying beside it. After a particularly vehement string of vicious assaults, I thought about being strong. Without warning, I grabbed the chair leg, and like a baseball player hitting one out of the park, I swung the leg, hitting her squarely on the temple.

Immediately, she fell to the ground from the force of the blow, a one-inch welt clearly visible. Oh God, I thought, I've killed her. In my child's mind, I was sure I was going to jail for murder. My neighborhood friends were open-mouthed and aghast at what I had just done.

Crying, I ran inside to tell my mother that I had killed Judy Rabideau. Out we both ran to find Judy sitting up holding her head. She wasn't dead, just reeling from the crushing blow to her head.

My mother applied ice to Judy's temple and called Judy's Dad to come down to survey the damage. Bud Rabideau was a huge, hulking man, and I was sure I was going to die. Surprisingly, he was kind to me and asked, "Why did you do that?" My answer was that my Dad told me to be strong.

Over the years, I have learned that strength takes many different forms. Well placed words, delivered with speed and accuracy, are just as effective as clobbering someone on the head.

And, you don't have to worry about going to jail.

Scars

After I got out of the shower this morning and was brushing my hair, my attention was drawn to my right earlobe where I have a quarter inch split. Sadly, my right earlobe looks exactly like a pig's foot. If you don't know what a pig's foot looks like, Google pictures of pigs' feet and you will understand. Not attractive on an earlobe. Not sure it is attractive on a pig, either. I thought about getting it surgically sutured, but decided against it. It is a distinctive mark of me, and, more importantly, a reminder of my past.

As I stared at my earlobe, I clearly remembered getting my ears pierced. In my family, ear piercing was not allowed. Growing up in an Italian-American community and living in a family fraught with prejudice, the feeling was that "only Guinea Catholics" got their ears pierced. Ear piercing was strictly forbidden. I didn't understand any of that, but I didn't push it. We had enough conflict in our house, and I chose my battles carefully.

My early college years were liberating in a way that I could never have imagined. I was away from a family dynamic that was restrictive, dark, and combative. Pledged to a sorority that was artistic, supportive, and not traditional for Greek life, I felt a freedom I had never felt before. Finally, I felt I was becoming my own person. No restrictions, no prejudice, no restraints.

Ear piercing was wildly popular in the late 60's. One Sunday, several of my sorority sisters and I were making breakfast in the kitchen. The cook had the weekend off, and we were on our own for meals. We talked about many things—guys, classes, makeup, and finally ear piercing. Two of my sorority sisters already had their ears pierced and showed me their amazing earrings. My sorority sister, Mary, said, "You know, Potter (she called me Potter even though my last name was not Potter), if you want your ears pierced, I can do that for you. I know how to do it!"

This gave me pause. But, yes, I wanted my ears pierced! No matter the family restriction. I was a new woman. Without hesitation, I said, "Mare, I would love that! Let's do it!"

Armed with ice, the largest sewing needle I had ever seen, and rubbing alcohol, Mary proceeded with all the skill of a surgeon. Now I can't say it didn't hurt. It did, but the thrill of independence and liberation overrode the pain of penetration. When it was over, she placed a stud in my ear. Done. And then, I said, "Do it again. I want two piercings in each ear. Put the next one below the first one." And so, she proceeded to pierce my ears again. Once done, she placed another stud in each of the new holes and declared herself a successful surgeon. I agreed.

In subsequent years, I filled the pierced holes with the most attractive and heavy earrings I could find. I loved it.

When I came home from college that year with not one, but two piercings in my ears, it did not go well. My mother told me that I looked like a Guinea slut. Now a newly liberated and confident woman, I said defiantly, "I don't care what you think," and moved on.

Over the years, the flirtation of one ear piercing with another consummated in a union. I woke up one morning to find the two as one, resulting in the pig's foot that exists today. It was and is the symbol of my liberation and newly found confidence, which was a long time coming.

Looking at the rest of my body after my shower, I focused on my left ankle. The two scars and broken blood vessels that exist today took me back to my freshman year in the dorm.

My roommate was a sweet girl. Overweight and insecure, she seemed unable to make the changes in herself that she desperately wanted to make. She was struggling and broken that year. One night, I came into our room and found her gone. Odd, I thought, because it was after the 11:00 curfew. I fell asleep and the next morning found her still gone, her bed unslept in.

Back in the late 60's on campus, this was a big deal. There were dorm monitors and doors were locked after 11:00 PM. While nobody made a bed check, it was required that you be in by 11:00. Nobody much violated this rule, especially my roommate. I was concerned and went to see our floor monitor. This was not like my roommate. She was a preacher's daughter and not inclined to break God's rules or anyone else's, either. After hours of checking with her parents and following as many leads as possible, we learned that she had run away from campus and taken a bus to Virginia to visit her brother, her refuge in times of trouble.

I was so relieved to know she was safe, I ran to the music building to tell my boyfriend, Sam, that she was ok. It was raining, and I was running. The slick soles of my shoes caused me to slip. With a thud, I fell on the concrete sidewalk. When I looked down at my left leg, my foot jutted to the left while my leg remained straight. This is bad, I thought. At that moment, my ankle didn't hurt as much as it probably should have. I was in shock, I suspect.

As luck, or lack of luck, would have it, nobody was around. I mean, nobody. I'm not sure how long I laid there in the rain. It probably wasn't that long, but felt like forever. As my leg began to throb, I glanced down the sidewalk. Someone was coming! I knew that walk. It was Sam! When he got to me, he knew I was in trouble. In the days before cell phones, he couldn't exactly call 911 from the rainy sidewalk. So, he did what was so typical of Sam. He carefully picked me up and carried me the three blocks to the hospital.

Once in the emergency room, the ER doctor proceeded to cut my pants off. Strangely, though I was in considerable pain, the first thought that went through my mind was, "Oh God, I haven't shaved my legs for a week!" You've heard the old mother adage that you should always wear clean underwear in case you are in an accident. Ever since the ankle incident, I do two things always. I make sure I have on clean underwear, and I make sure I shave my legs in case somebody has to cut my pants off.

Since I had recently eaten, my ankle had to be reset without the benefit of anesthesia. Told to bite down on a tongue depressor and take a deep breath, the doctor forcefully pulled my ankle and put it back in the proper place. It was back in place, but the damage had been done. I was taken in to surgery the next morning where two pins were inserted to piece my ankle back together.

After five months of navigating campus on crutches, my cast was removed. Some things that are broken take longer to heal than others. That May, I lost my cast, and I lost my Sam. The three scars—two external and one internal- continue to be the symbols of all that was broken that year.

Continuing my after-shower inventory, my eyes next

focused on my abdomen. A seven-inch C-section scar smiled back at me.

I had my first child at 28, an older age at that time to be having a first child. Healthy and athletic, I navigated my way through my pregnancy with the skill of an accomplished road runner. My pregnancy was uneventful until the seventh month. During one of my check-ups with the obstetrician, I was told that my baby was in the breech position, poised to come out feet and butt first. Though this could cause complications, he told me not to worry. He said it was very common for the baby to turn back into the correct position on its own. I certainly hoped so.

In my 9th month, my doctor was happy to report that the baby had, indeed, turned itself around and was ready to come into the world head first.

In the early morning hours on the day I delivered, my water broke while I as peacefully sleeping. I knew soon the contractions would begin. Now, I am not a hospital kind of girl, and so I chose to stay at home until my contractions spoke strongly enough to me to tell me it was time to go. I was at home for four hours in labor before it was time to take the twenty-minute drive to the hospital.

When I arrived and was examined by the doctor, I was told that the baby was in the breech position again and that I would need an emergency C-section. Within minutes, I was prepped and taken to surgery. No Bob. He wasn't allowed in, and I was on my own. I was transferred from the gurney and placed on an ice-cold surgery table. There was no pillow and no blanket to keep me warm. I was freezing and in full blown labor.

The surgery nurse, being somewhat inept, was unable to place the IV in my arm to begin the pre-anesthesia process.

After several unsuccessful tries, she summoned the anesthesiologist. From my vantage point on that cold surgery table, when he entered the room, he looked for all the world like he had been on an all-night bender and stumbled into the OR. He was bleary-eyed and his hands shook so badly, I thought he would never get the IV in. This wasn't going well, was it?

When I woke up from the surgery, I was unable to breathe. The anesthesia, I was told later, had worn off but the paralytic had not. My body was paralyzed, preventing me from taking a breath, but I was fully awake. I heard the anesthesiologist say, "Come on now. Just try to breathe. I'm going to remove the tracheal tube."

At that moment, I was suddenly above him, watching him remove the tracheal tube and apply a bag bulb mask to aid in my breathing. I was fascinated with his efforts to revive me and felt a peace that I had never experienced before. I don't know how long I watched him from above, since time during this event was clearly suspended. What I do recall was returning to the surgical table and feeling the nurse massaging my uterus to expel the placenta. With more than a hundred stitches in my abdomen, you can bet at that point I could feel some pain. I didn't get to see my baby girl until 12 hours after she was born, and it was a glorious occasion.

Six weeks later, before my post-partum examination, with a marker, I drew two eyes above my smiley C-section scar. The doctor at the exam, of course, laughed, and I did, too, but the smiley face was my own private commentary.

When I look at my smiley scar today, I still imagine the eyes I drew above it. That face is the face of gratitude that I got to raise my daughter into the beautiful woman she has become, and for me to have been able to continue on my path of life.

Looking in the mirror, my eyes next travelled to my neck where a three-inch scar reflected back at me. When I was in the corporate world and colleagues would ask me how I got that scar, I whimsically told them that I had a cut-throat job. The truth was slightly more traumatic and infinitely more positive.

I used to take back roads to work. Not one for hectic interstates or congested roads, I loved my backroad route. I had a beautiful view of the foothills and the vast open space. The closer I got to Boulder, more houses appeared and more streets jutted up against the 63rd Street route that I took.

One morning on my way to the monitoring center, my mind was on the work day and the felons we would be monitoring. Traveling ahead, I noticed a white Mazda sports car stopped at the stop sign waiting for me to pass. Nice car for what appeared to be a nineteen or twenty-year-old girl. When I got within fifteen feet of passing by that stop sign, suddenly the Mazda darted out in front of me, trying to make it across the road before I passed.

Having never been in a car accident, I had no idea how time slows to a crawl in the moments before impact. I remember having the time to think through what was about to happen. I thought, if I keep going straight (there wasn't enough time to brake to avoid impact) and I hit this girl on the driver's side door, I am likely going to kill her. If I turn my car to the left and cross the opposite lane of traffic, I could likely get hit myself.

In the end, there was only one right decision. I veered my car to the left, hit her front quarter panel before crossing the opposite lane of traffic, and crashed down an embankment into an open space in front of someone's house. Exiting my car and climbing back up the embankment, I crossed the road to see if the girl was hurt. Except for the damage to her car, there was no lasting damage to her. She was shaken, but not hurt.

As I walked back to my car, I had the chance to really observe what had just happened. When I drove down the embankment, I managed to navigate my car between an electrical box and a telephone box, before crashing through a fence. The distance between the electrical box and telephone box was so close, if I was lucky, which I was, I had no more than six inches on either side of my car to make it through without crashing into them. I'm pretty sure angels were guiding me that morning.

We called the State Patrol and the officer asked me how I felt. I said fine, considering what had just happened. He said, "I think I should call an ambulance for you and have you checked out at the hospital. You are probably in shock and not able to assess your own injuries." True to form, I declined and said I was fine. When my daughter came to pick me up, she wasn't buying it. She said," Mom, we're going to the hospital." I was put in a cervical collar and treated for severe shoulder harness burns from the impact. A year later, after experiencing chronic neck pain, I underwent a cervical fusion to repair the damage to my neck.

When I look at that scar today, I smile because my actions that day probably saved a young girl's life. And… it doesn't get any better than that.

Next, my odyssey took me to one of my most recent acquisitions—scars on my abdomen. This year, I made the acquaintance of four new friends, the quadruplets. The act of carrying a 1x4x6 inch piece of plywood like I was a twenty-year-old resulted in the birth of the quads. I can't say that I was attached to them. They hurt, and I was glad to be done with them. Hernia surgery, happily, removed them from my life.

Two weeks after the surgery, I removed the butterfly tape covering the incisions and was surprised by what I saw. On either side of my navel, itself the site of an umbilical hernia repair, were two one-half inch vertical incisions. It was distinctly the binary code 101. In base 10, binary code 101 is the number 5. Just for fun, I looked up the significance of the number 5 in numerology. Here is what I discovered:

"The number 5 is the number of manifestation. It is the number of the five elements—earth, air, water, fire, and ether. Within the five elements are all the components necessary for creative manifestation. 5 is a very free-spirited, creative number. The spiritual essence of the number 5 aligns to freedom, to feel the freedom to pursue that which fills your heart with purposeful joy and bliss. 5 is a doing number, representing faith in action, and having a mindful connection to the synergy of the forces of nature."

With my new scars, daily, I am happily reminded that creative manifestation is my destiny, and to pay attention to what they are telling me. These scars, despite my clear dislike of the quadruplets, send the most hopeful and positive message of them all.

Finally, my body odyssey took me again to my abdomen, where my most recent and most prominent scar proudly displays itself. A vertical railroad track (so named because of the length of the incision and the position of the staple scars), it runs from under my Xiphoid bone to six inches below. My navel, in the middle of the track, looks like a train station where passengers wait for the next arriving train.

On a Thursday early in December, my daily dog park adventure completed, I decided to go shopping. After two hours at Walmart and Costco, I began the drive home. I wasn't in the car for more than five minutes before my stomach began to hurt—really hurt! Or at least I thought it was my stomach. Ouch, I thought. What is that about??

Distractedly driving home, my mind was on the pain and what might be causing it. Never a big eater, I tried to think of what might be going on. The day before, I had eaten nothing. At noon that day, I decided I needed to eat something, so I made myself some chicken, quinoa and rice. Hmm. Maybe the chicken wasn't cooked enough. Maybe it was some sort of food poisoning

When I got home, I just sat in my recliner, something I rarely do. Ouch! The cramps were severe. Nothing I tried would stop the pain. As is my way, I thought, well, this will pass. Maybe if I just rest, it will go away. That evening, the pain was so severe, I couldn't sleep in my bed. Escaping to my recliner, I fitfully slept through the night.

At 4:00 in the morning, I texted my dog park friend, Vivianne, to tell her I wouldn't be going to the dog park in the morning. You have to understand something. I never cancel our dog park mornings together unless the weather is too severe. For 45 minutes in the morning, they are my escape and my refuge. They keep me sane. A kindred spirit on so many levels, Vivianne and I laugh, enjoy our dogs' freedom, and yes, sometimes we share each other's pain as we ride the Alzheimer's train together, she with her father, and me with my friend and roommate. So, no, I would never say I'm not going.

The rest of that Friday morning, the pain was intolerable. Vivianne texted me and asked me how I was doing.

"Not good," I said. "You should go to the doctor!" she said. Reluctantly, I agreed. I called my doctor's office and got an appointment with the nurse practitioner for that day. The nurse practitioner agreed with me, it probably was food poisoning. She said it should be better in the next day, but if it wasn't, I should go to urgent care or the ER. Ok, I thought again, this will probably pass.

A second night in the recliner brought me fitful sleep, but no relief from the pain. But, by mid-morning, I did feel some relief! That Saturday morning, I texted Vivianne to tell her I was better and that I was probably turning the corner on this thing, whatever it was.

And I was better. Two hours later, the cramps were back with a vengeance. Hurting and frustrated, I drove myself to the urgent care in town. After all that effort, I was disappointed to find that the urgent care was closed!! I didn't have the energy or the stamina to drive myself to the ER in Ft. Collins, a fifteen-minute drive away.

So…I drove home. Before I went to my place, I stopped in to see my neighbor, Marla. A retired nurse, she was wise, and I trusted her judgement completely. I told her that I suspected food poisoning, mostly because I had no idea what it could be otherwise. She listened carefully to what I said and asked me a number of questions. "You know, Porter, this could be something else. You don't want to fool with this. I'll take you to the ER." Knowing that she was going to her granddaughter's volleyball game that afternoon, I just couldn't impose on her, even though I really hurt. So, I said, "No, I'll be fine. I'll just rest and if it isn't better in the morning, I'll drive to the ER in Ft. Collins."

At 6:00 PM, I texted Vivianne to tell her the cramps were back with a vengeance. I have a high pain tolerance, but this was nuts. Her response in her text message was, "Don't mess around with this too long! You should go to the ER. I will drive you!!!" Not wanting to impose on her Saturday night family time, I said, "You're so sweet. Hopefully, I won't have to go. If it hurts in the morning, I'll go, and I'll let you know."

Ten minutes later, Vivianne called me. "Don't mess with this!" she said. "I'll be there in five minutes!" "I look terrible," I said. "I don't want to scare you!" "I don't care what you look like!" she said. "I'll be there in five minutes!"

And so, she came. Together, we drove to the ER in Loveland, closer than the ER in Ft. Collins. While she parked her car, I walked into the ER. I can't say I wasn't scared. I was. The Medical Center of the Rockies took me back to an ER room quickly. Vivianne was with me soon.

The ER nurse asked me a bunch of embarrassing questions, especially in front of my friend who would not leave my side. "Did you have a bowel movement? Did you throw up?" he asked. "No," I said. "I felt nauseous but couldn't throw up. And no, I couldn't eat or have a bowel movement. "Ok," he said. "We are going to do a CAT scan of your abdomen." And so, after a venous port was inserted, I was off to have a CAT scan.

We had arrived at the ER at 7:00 PM. By 10:00, the CAT scan results were read. I just kept thinking about the time Vivianne was missing with her family. "Stop," she said. "It's fine!" When one of the doctors arrived (there were five in all for this event), he sat down in front of me, his eyes as big as quarters, and said, "I can't believe you are sitting up like this! You have a severe bowel blockage, most likely caused by scar tissue from your hernia surgery, that will require emergency surgery. It is about to rupture, so we may have to perform an ileostomy, a temporary bowel bypass." I knew what an ileostomy was, and I cried. So, with that, the two primary surgeons and three radiologists reviewed my CAT scan again. My primary ER surgeon told me that, while my CAT scan was difficult to interpret, they agreed, after an intensive consultation together, they could fix this by removing eight inches of my colon and attaching my remaining colon to my small intestine. Thank God, I thought. No ileostomy, no colostomy. No bypass to the outside of my body!! I was blessed. And so, at 11:30 at night, I was whisked off to surgery, my amazing friend at my side, holding my hand and encouraging me that it would all be ok. She called my family and didn't get home until well after midnight that night.

After the surgery, I spent five days in the hospital recovering. Bored and restless, I walked the halls and wrote a story about my iv pole, my constant companion for four of the five days I was in the hospital. It helped me pass the time. The doctors told me that if I had waited another day, my colon would have ruptured, and they weren't sure what the consequences would have been. Sepsis, a long struggle, and death probably could have been the outcome. I kept thinking how blessed I was to have a good friend who insisted I go to the ER and who stayed with me through everything.

People come into our lives for reasons we will never really know. Sometimes it is to teach us life lessons. Sometimes it is to teach us tolerance and kindness, and to give us hope. Sometimes it is to share a difficult journey together. And sometimes, it is to literally save our lives by their caring actions. Vivianne saved me in so many ways, and, for that, I will be eternally grateful.

This odyssey of my body has reminded me of many, many things. Our bodies are the road map of our lifetime experiences. Every scar and every flaw has a story to tell. It is good to re-read that story from time to time. It is, after all, the story of us.

The Shovel

Finally! A day off. To be more accurate, it was a day out of the office. There was no such thing as a day off for me. As the Director of Monitoring Operations for a home arrest monitoring company, I was on call twenty-four hours a day, three hundred-sixty-five days a year. In the days before everyone had cell phones, I wore a pager around the clock. If systems malfunctioned or some paroled felon went on the lam and caused trouble, I was contacted, no matter the time of day or day of the week. Days out of the office, with time just to myself, were rare.

On this day, I decided to place landscape timbers in my front yard to border the shrubs and flowers I had planted. At 77 degrees with a clear sky, it was a great day to enjoy the sunshine, the solitude, and a good yard project. The neighborhood was so quiet, drilling holes in the landscape timbers and pounding the anchoring spikes into them echoed loudly. It was a much-needed retreat from the seamier side of life that had become my reality.

As I grabbed a second landscape timber to put in place, I had a feeling that my solitude was going to be broken. A side glance confirmed this as a tall, dark skinned man walked up my driveway and approached me.

"Hi, ma'am," he said, overly-grinning. "How are you today?" In my mind, I thought, I was just wonderful until you got here, though I didn't say that. "I'm just fine. What can I do for you?"

Quickly, he said, "I noticed you have a couple of stains on your driveway, maybe oil or something else that has seeped into your concrete. I have just the thing that will take those stains out. It is a state-of-the-art concrete cleaner for just this kind of thing. Would you let me show you what it can do?"

Ok, since he had already broken my peaceful reverie, I said, "Sure, show me," with no intent whatsoever on purchasing anything. After he sprayed his concrete cleaner and let it sit for a minute or two, I saw a slight reduction in the obviousness of the driveway stain.

"That's good," I said, "but I'm not interested." With that, he flashed a toothy grin at me and moved closer. "This is the best cleaner on the market. I know you would just love it. If you bought some and applied it in repeated applications, I know you would be pleased with the results."

"Thank you for the demonstration," I said," but I am not interested. "Thank you for your time." Thinking that he would get the hint and leave, instead he moved closer to me in the driveway. "I don't want you to miss out," he said. "I know that you would love this product. You seem to be a woman who likes things clean and neat and tidy, and this product will please you."

"I appreciate your demonstration, and your sales pitch," I said, "but I am not interested and just want to get back to my yard project." Instead of saying thank you ma'am for your time and walking away, again he moved closer to me, clearly violating my personal space.

We all have personal space rules. Close colleagues at work get the two-foot rule. Friends generally get the one-foot rule, depending on how close we are. Really close friends, loved ones, and family have no restrictions. In fact, the closer, the better. This guy was clearly violating my space rules.

Yet again, I said, "I really appreciate it, but I am not interested. Hope you have a nice day." With that, he moved closer to me than the close friend and family space rule. His actions were an egregious violation of my space, so finally, I said, "I want you to leave, now!"

What was it with this guy? He moved forward yet again, and I quickly backed up. "Look, buddy," I said, "I think I made it pretty clear that I don't want driveway cleaner. I just want to get back to my project."

I took a second to assess my fear gage. Did I think this guy was going to attack me? No, I really didn't. He was salesman-pushy, ignorant of space rules, didn't know when to quit talking, but basically harmless, I decided tentatively.

And so, he started to talk again, six inches from my face. "I really think you should try this cleaner. After several applications, I know you would be pleased with the results." Geez, what was it going to take to get this guy to back off and go away?

By my own admission, I am something of a control freak. I don't particularly like surprises, although, I know they can happen. That, after all, is life. But, as a rule, I like to plan my days and look forward to executing my plans to completion. A day like this was so rare, and I was so enjoying the sunshine and the solitude, I began to feel some strong resentment building up in me. I am a woman who is used to taking control of situations. Silver-tongued often, I am used to resolving issues politely and calmly by talking and expect what I ask for will happen. Not this time.

"Look," I said, feeling the resentment for lost time continuing to build in me. "I have asked you politely to leave, and you just keep talking. If you don't leave now, I am calling the police." With that, he still didn't budge and grinned at me.

Frustrated, I bolted up the driveway, and went to my front door to go inside to call the police. Keep in mind— these were the land-line days. There were no easy-reach cell phones, so I had to go inside to call. As I reached the front door and turned the door knob, nothing happened. Locked!! AARG! I forgot that I had locked the front door and exited out the back door so that I could retrieve my tools from the shed to complete my project. While my fear gage said he was harmless, still, a voice in me said don't go through the gate to the back door. He just might follow you.

Anger, and the resulting violence, can take many forms. There are those who are so angry with the world in general and, specifically their place in the world, that they will strike out indiscriminately at anyone, however anonymous, to right the wrongs that have been done to them. There are slighted lovers who feel such pain that they want to harm the one who hurt them. And there are others who are completely frustrated that some unknown someone derailed their plans and the time lost could not be regained. I was clearly the latter.

Violence is not in my nature. A counselor and teacher, my methods of resolution are always through calm, rational talk. Hurting someone is just not part of my emotional make-up. But, today, something snapped. Feeling so out of control and vulnerable, I was suddenly overwhelmed. I felt inappropriate rage and anger.

Since I couldn't call the police without going to the back door, I now looked around the front yard to see what I could do. Sitting beside my landscape timbers was a shovel. Running to the project site, I picked up the shovel. "If you don't get the hell out of here, I will hit you with this shovel!" Sad to say, at that moment, I meant it and could have done real harm to him.

Freeze frame—Though angry, wild, and out of control, I stepped outside of myself and had a clear view of me wildly wielding the shovel, hair standing on end, and frustration steam shooting out of my nostrils. I was clearly willing and able to assault this man. For what, I asked myself? Because he was overzealous and didn't know when to quit talking?

Seeing the violence in my nature now, the driveway cleaner salesman quickly backed away and walked into the street. Clearly alarmed, he said, "There's no need to be violent!"

The sad part about this incident is that I could actually have hit him and wanted to hit him. The reason I didn't is multifaceted. The voice in my head told me several things, obviously at just the right time. If you hit this man, you will lose your job. Home Arrest Operations Mangers could never have felony or misdemeanor charges against them. If you actually hit him, you could have one to twenty-five years in prison for aggravated assault and battery charges, if convicted. These things resonated in my mind. Spending twenty-five years in prison sharing a cell with Big Bertha didn't appeal to me. I wasn't a prison kind of girl.

Jails and prisons are filled with people who have committed momentary acts of aggression that they later regretted. I am glad I listened to that voice inside of me and didn't become one of them.

Over the years, I have talked about this incident with my friends and my girls. We laugh, but we know that some events can bring any of us to the point of out-of-character, insane actions. Among my close friends and family, we share, that while I am not a violent person at all, my intense feelings are now measured in "shovels up". It is my mood gage. One shovel up, my frustration and anger are manageable. Two shovels up—DON'T START! Three shovels up—RUN!! Fortunately for me, and for them, three shovels up is a rare occurrence.

As for that day, after my encounter with the driveway cleaning guy, I returned to the serenity of my much, much-needed yard project. Happily, the most aggressive act I committed that day was hitting landscape spikes on the head—hard—with a hammer. Pretty harmless, in the scheme of things.

And… nobody went to prison.

A Visit from Trinity

Seventy degrees with a slight breeze strong enough to make the young pecan trees behind the house sway in synchronized movement, it was a cloudless blue-sky day in late November, the kind of day perfect for putting up hooks in anticipation of hanging the Christmas lights on the house.

I grabbed the light-weight aluminum ladder and carried it to the front window. As I surveyed the house, plotting the positioning of the light hooks, I couldn't help but reflect on the events of the past seven months. A February longing for change spawned a series of events that once set in motion raced forward at a dizzying pace. Where would I want to move? Close to the ocean. What kind of weather? Warm, tropical, but with an occasional 40 degrees to remind me of Colorado days. What kind of town? Artistic, small, safe, welcoming. My friend Nancy's sister had lived in Fairhope, Alabama. A former colleague lived in Fairhope. How about Fairhope? An internet search sold me, but I had to see for myself. The April visit didn't disappoint. Fairhope it was.

Fix up the Colorado house, list it, show it, sell it, close it. My life was upside down. After 30 years in Colorado, I was moving on. After a tearful goodbye to my daughters and grandchildren, I loaded the Scion bus with three cats and a 100 plus pound chocolate lab with a heart condition to drive the 1600 miles to my new home.

The sun warmed my face as I dipped the white cloth in the sudsy water. This window sill had to be washed before I applied the "damage free" clear hooks for hanging the lights. No drilling holes. A quick stick and they were up.

The wrung water from the cloth echoed in the bucket. Quiet. So much quiet in this neighborhood, especially on my street. Such a contrast from my Colorado home where cars raced on the highway behind my house. At times, it seemed as though no one else lived here at all. It was like a child's playhouse neighborhood where no one ever appeared until the little girl who owned the playhouse placed someone exactly where she wanted them to be.

I climbed the ladder to reach the top of the window. Late November, 70 degrees. My Colorado friends wouldn't believe it. It was so…

"Hey!" The sound of another voice nearly sent me tumbling off the ladder.

"Hey! Hey!" I turned to see a little girl of 7 or 8 ditch her hot pink bike at the curb and bolt into the center of my front lawn.

"Hey! Are you my teacher?

"Well, no," I said. "But I used to be a teacher. "

"No, I guess you're not. She has long hair down to here." She tapped her shoulders and smiled quizzically as she studied my face.

"You're old. I go to Newton school. We just talked about old people at school. We don't have school at Thanksgiving. I'm supposed to help an old person. My teacher says it is good to help old people. What are you doing? I can help you."

"I'm putting up hooks so I can hang my Christmas lights in a couple of weeks," I said. "No, I don't need any help, but thank you anyway."

"I live down that street," she said pointing. "I'm Trinity. What kind of hooks do you have? Where are you putting them? I can do hooks. Do you like Turkey? We are having a Turkey at Thanksgiving."

"Thank you, Sweetie. But I'm fine. There's only a few of these to put up, and I can finish them."

Glancing at her mismatched clothes, disheveled blonde hair, and hot pink bike ditched at the curb, I knew this was a little girl who knew exactly what she wanted. One look at that face, and I knew I was in trouble. So much for the serenity of this November afternoon.

Galloping toward the ladder, Trinity said, "Let's take them out of the package. We can line them up here. You take some, and I'll take some. But I'm small, so I have to do the bottom. You do the top, but don't step on the hooks when you climb up there. If you fall, I can tell someone, but I can't catch you or anything. But I do have to help an old person because Ms. Crutcher says we should because it is nice, and we should practice doing it. I have to help someone before we go back to school Monday."

With that, there was no saying no to her. Damn. She was cute and all, but you have to understand something about me. I am a project person. A Type A project loner who knows exactly how she wants her projects done. I plan and organize and triple check my work.

In a flash, Trinity grabbed the package of hooks, ripped open the side, and dumped all of them on a step of the ladder. "'K. What are these things?" she said, pointing to the adhesive strips to be applied to the inside and outside of the hooks.

"See, this side is red, and the other side is black," I said. "You have to peel this red side off and stick it on the hook.

Then you peel the black side off and stick the hook here on the window." Carefully, I peeled off the strips to show her what to do. Measuring the distance I wanted them to be apart, I pressed the hook to the window ledge. "See," I said.

"'K. You get on the ladder and do the top. I'm doing here."

Without hesitation, she grabbed the adhesive, peeled off the black side, stuck it on the hook, peeled off the red side and stuck it on the ledge. Within seconds, the hook fell to the ground.

Looking down from the top of the ladder, I said, "I think you might have gotten the strips mixed up. I can show you again." As I started down the ladder, she grabbed another hook and announced, "I can do hooks. You do the top."

With that, she began tearing off strips, papers flying, and sticking hooks on the ledge. This time the adhesive was just right. I climbed back to the top of the ladder, focusing on the section Trinity had assigned to me. Measuring, peeling, and sticking, I had completed two hooks before she announced, "I'm done. What else can we do?"

I climbed back down the ladder to inspect her work. She was, indeed, done. All ten hooks stuck in a mismatch of directions and distances. "Well, thank you, sweetie," I said, trying to conceal my horror at the mess she had made of my project.

"'K. Let's go inside." Unabashed, she headed for the front door and opened it. Quickly following on her heels, I entered the front hallway. Dropped to her knees, Trinity was petting Molly, my 20-year-old Siamese who loved everybody.

"Your cat's old, too." Quickly standing up, Trinity glanced around the house. I had never seen her, in the whole hour of her life that I had known her, stand so still. The look on her face said it all. Although she said nothing,

I could crawl inside that mind of hers and see her thinking. "Cool. This is what an old person's house looks like inside. I have to tell Ms. Crutcher."

The calm lasted all of 10 seconds when she said, "Got any cookies?" And off she went to the kitchen.

Now, normally, I have tons of cookies in my house. But not this day. "No, hon. I don't have any cookies today. But sometime when you come back, I'll give you some cookies that I baked."

Staring at the pantry, she said, "Let's make them now. Where's the stuff?" Instantly, my mind went to "that place" and played a video of a cookie project in my kitchen with Trinity. I nearly fainted, but recovered quickly enough to say, "Sweetie, I really need to go back outside to finish what I was doing. But you can come back sometime."

With one old person project safely under her belt, Trinity grinned and dashed out the front door. Righting her hot pink bike and stabilizing her balance, she hollered back, "'K. Bye"

Trinity never returned, not even with the promise of cookies. I think of her often. I learned a couple of things about myself from her visit. I never really thought about it before, but I *am* old, and I'm ok with that. Although, frequently I remind myself that to a 7-year-old, anyone over the age of 12 is old.

I also learned that if a 7-year-old brought my Type A project world down around my knees, I could survive.

And finally, I learned that if I could turn my life upside down and drive across the country with a sick old dog and three cats, I could learn to leave Trinity's crookedy old light hooks right there on the window ledge where she put them.

The Runner

I have been a runner for as long as I can remember. I took up long distance running in my early thirties, but I was a runner long before that.

Sometimes, I imagine I am at a runners' group meeting, introducing myself for the first time. "Hi, I'm Porter, and I am an emotional runner. When feelings get too strong or emotional attachments become too important in my life, I run to the closest shelter to shield me from potential hurt."

I recently saw a movie called The Last Word. The main character, Harriot Lauler, engages the talents of a young obituary writer to write her obituary before she has died. Lately, I have been wondering what my obituary would look like if it was written today. "Porter Penn, a talented musician, writer, and teacher died on Monday. A lifelong runner, she leaves behind two daughters, two granddaughters, and a legacy of aborted emotional relationships. Although she touched many lives, she will not truly be missed."

As a young child, when the emotional frenzy of a dysfunctional family reached an unbearable peak, mentally I would escape into a snow globe my Dad bought for me on one of his business trips. Safely inside the shaken snow globe, the falling snow shielded me from the white heat of emotion. I went there often.

As one would expect, in middle school and high school, I experienced the highs and lows of adolescent passion. Fickle and unpredictable, it frightened me. When the highs got too high and the lows too low, I did what I did best. I ran. I ran to the arms of Rose, my bassoon, and the safety of classical music and scholarship. Rose was safe. As long as I breathed life into her, we were one. Predictable, constant, and joined.

I met Sam when I was a freshman in college. A fellow musician, he was smart, talented, creative, and funny. He lit up my world just being around him. We spent every minute together. We had classes together, ate together, and went to fraternity parties and football games. We roller skated through the indoor commons area, an act strictly forbidden, and laughed until we cried each time we did it. I loved him, and for once in my life, I didn't run. I couldn't imagine my life without him.

I knew the summer break would be hard. He lived three hours away from me. Each holding summer jobs, we both knew the times we had together would be few.

Several days before the end of the term, Sam and I were having dinner at a drive-in. We were talking, eating, and listening to the radio. When the Beatles song "We Can Work It Out" played, he stopped talking and said, "I want you to listen closely to this song." Well, I had heard it before, and liked it, so I listened. Later, when we were at his apartment, he said, "There's something I need to tell you. I've been meaning to, but I didn't know how to tell you. I didn't want to lose what we have together." And so, he told me the story. In his senior year of high school, his girlfriend became pregnant. Being a man of character and dictated by the norms of the day, he did the right thing. He married her. My Sam had a wife and a child.

I looked into his eyes and the punch of this reality knocked the breath out of me. The world I created around him was completely shattered. There was no "working it out", as the Beatles said. It was the 1960's, and I was the other woman.

So, I ran. Ran from him and from the safety of Rose and music. I changed my major and left the music program. I just couldn't be around him every day. It hurt too much. I was devastated and angry. No Sam, no Rose, no music, no safe haven.

During the next college years, I dated off and on, but was always careful not to have expectations, and certainly no emotional attachments. But in my junior year, I met Bob—the guy who looked like Eddie, my roommate's boyfriend. We were lab partners in biology class. He was sweet, easy on the eyes, and someone I perceived as stable—someone I could count on to always be there. I wasn't in love, but he was a safe place to run to. Or so I thought. Seventeen years and two children later, I discovered I was mistaken. Cheating was not something I could tolerate—ever.

Running again, I sought a new safe haven. I threw myself into my work. Unable to find a teaching job because I had too many degrees and too much experience for school districts to afford, l took a job as the Director of a failing preschool. I loved it!! I had complete autonomy to run the center as if it was my own business. I controlled the finances, the marketing, the curriculum, and the customer relations. In three months, the center was full and the finances were in the black. I had run to the right place.

It was there I met Nancy, my daughter's pre-school teacher. Nancy, running from an abusive marriage, and I found a safe haven in each other's friendship. We remained best friends and roommates until this year. Over the years, we each dipped our toes in the emotional waters of outside attachment, but always retreated back to the safe haven of our friendship. No expectations. No hurt. This year, Nancy ran away with Alzheimer's, and I, too, now find myself running again. Writing, for now, is as good a place to run any, it seems.

Truth be told, I am tired of running. As a running addict and, ironically, a counselor myself, I know all of the advice about my condition. If you don't let yourself experience the highs and lows of emotional experience, you are on the ride, but miss the journey. If you run because of potential hurt, you miss the ecstasy of those special moments, however fleeting they might be.

There is a difference between knowing and KNOWING. When you know, you intellectually understand. When you KNOW, you understand in your head and your gut simultaneously. Knowing leaves you thoughtful; KNOWING leaves you changed.

Despite my addiction to running, I now KNOW. I am ready for change. As with any addiction, each day will be a struggle. The urge to run will be strong and seductive. I KNOW this and will keep pushing forward. For once, after so many years, I just don't want to miss the journey.

Trinity Revisited

Rounding the corner onto Bonham Avenue, I stared down at my running shoes. I loved walking in this neighborhood. In fact, I loved everything about this neighborhood. The quiet, the wide streets, the charming brick houses with oversized lots, the open-space lined with rows of crepe myrtles. And, yes, the quiet.

A February longing for change six years ago found me crossing the country from Colorado to the Gulf Coast. My new home was Fairhope, Alabama, the best kept secret on the Gulf. A haven for artists and writers, it was a Norman Rockwell painting of small-town America, a place to start over, to make it count, and to become anyone I wanted to become! I needed this. Needed the challenge, needed the hope, needed to feel that my life was what I chose to make of it. Here, the opportunities were now endless.

The sound of the school bus brought me back from thought. Glancing up to the opposite side of the street, I saw a young girl with a backpack walking an imaginary line from the holly bush to the mailbox and back. She was mouthing something, as if singing, although I could hear no sound.

Squinting to get a closer look at her face, I thought, Trinity? Could it be? She lived on this street somewhere. Could that be her? She looked different—taller. Her hair was combed and her clothes matched. I walked closer to get a better look. I knew that face. It WAS her!

Cautiously, I crossed the street and walked in her direction. I didn't want to scare her, but wanted to say hi, to see if she remembered coming to my house, and, yes, to see if she was real. As I approached the mailbox, she lifted her head in my direction and smiled broadly.

"Are you Trinity?" I said.

She nodded yes.

"Do you remember me?"

"Yes," she said. "We put up hooks together"

"That's right. Last year. I wrote a story about you."

"You did? About me?" she said, grinning so broadly and squinting, I could no longer see the color of her eyes. "Why did you do that?"

"I liked you. Thought you were different. Thought you were interesting. And, I wanted to remember your visit to my house."

How could I forget? It had been a cloudless, blue-sky kind of day in late November. I was putting up hooks in anticipation of hanging outside Christmas lights and thinking about how jealous my Colorado friends would be that I was basking in 70-degree weather. The neighborhood was so quiet, and I was lost in reverie when a young voice hollered, "Hey! Hey!" The sound of another voice so startled me that I nearly fell off the ladder I was on.

I turned to see a little girl of 7 or 8 ditch her hot pink bike at the curb and bolt into my front yard. Grinning broadly, this disheveled mismatched mess was clearly on a mission. Chattering a-mile-a minute and pushing her way into my life, she was here to complete a homework assignment her teacher had given her to help an old person. I was there, and I guess I filled the bill.

After telling her numerous times that I didn't need any help putting up the hooks for the Christmas lights, I finally gave up. She was so cute and so determined, I thought I would help her out with her classroom assignment. As a Type A project nerd, it was hard for me to share my carefully calculated project plan with anyone, much less a seven-year old. While I was calculated and exact, she was wild and uninhibited. The result was a misplaced and crooked nightmare.

My carefully laid out project a mess, she ran unabash-edly into my house looking for another project for us to work on and announced that my cat, whom she greeted in the foyer, was old, too. Next, she wanted to make cookies. Normally, I would have tons of cookies in my house, but not this day. My mind flashed to a video of Trinity and me making cookies in my kitchen, and I nearly fainted. Composing myself, I said, "Sweetie, I need to finish what I was doing outside, but you can come back."

After our encounter, I never saw Trinity again. Her assignment complete, there was no need for a return visit to see me. I had learned a lot about myself from her visit. I learned that I *was* old, and I was, surprisingly, ok with that. I learned that if things didn't exactly go exactly as I had planned them, I could survive. Seemed like great material for a story, so I wrote one.

Over the months, I shared my story with my writing class and neighborhood friends. Trinity began to take on a life of her own. She was a symbol of change and a symbol of innocence. Sometimes I wondered if she was real at all, or if I just sketched her in my mind as a way to personify the changes I was seeking and the acceptance of the stage of life I was in.

So, here she was—a year and a half later, taller and not so messy. And she was real.

"Know what?" I said to Trinity. "I sent the story to a publisher. If it gets it gets put in a book, you'll be famous!" Grinning, she shrugged her shoulders and dug the toe of her shoe in the grass. "One thing, though, I didn't know your teacher's name from last year, so I just made up a name."

"Ms. Crutcher," Trinity said. "Ms. Crutcher is her name."

"I'll bet she was proud of you for helping an old person!"

"I don't know," she said. Sensing that I was making her feel uncomfortable, I said, "I am going to finish my walk now. I'm so glad I got to see you again. Hope I get to make you famous!"

Smiling, I walked down the street away from her. Having seen Trinity again, I thought it might be fun to go to the Newton School and give Ms. Crutcher a copy of the story.

A week later, I did just that.

As I walked into the Newton school office, I said, "Hi, I have a strange request. I wrote a story about a girl named Trinity. Sorry, I don't know her last name, but she was in Ms. Crutcher's class last year. I would appreciate it if you would give my story to Ms. Crutcher." Happy about my decision to come to the school, I handed the Admin the story, a note to Ms. Crutcher, and my email address.

"I know Trinity," she said, "and I will be happy to give this story to Ms. Crutcher."

Two days later, while I was sitting on my porch after finishing extensive yard work, the doorbell rang. Hot and sweaty, I walked to the front door and opened it. Standing in front of me was Trinity and another little girl I hadn't met before. As I glanced beyond them into my front yard, I saw two electric bikes laying on the lawn. Trinity's, of course, was the pink one, a third-grade version of the hot pink bike she had ditched at my curb a year and a half ago. Her eyes slits from grinning so broadly, Trinity said, "Hi, again. This is my best friend, Jasmine. She wanted to meet you. I told her that you wrote a story about me, and that I was going to be famous. She wants you to make her famous, too."

I wanted to laugh at this third-grade, innocent logic, but didn't, of course, and said, "Would you like to come in? We'll go out on the back porch."

For about a half an hour, we talked about school, the neighborhood kids, and their electric bikes, clearly a source of pride for both of them. Finally, Trinity said, "I saw Ms. Crutcher. I was eating lunch, and she came over to my table. I thought I was in trouble, but she told me that you came to Newton School to give her your story about me. I was happy, and she liked it, too. Wanna do something?"

"What would you like to do," I said, hoping that she wouldn't say let's make cookies.

"I dunno," she said.

Ever the child magnet, my housemate and friend, Nancy, said, "You wanna play hide and seek?" Giggling, both Trinity and Jasmine said, "Yes!!!!"

And so, here we were, two older former teachers and two third graders setting off on a hide and seek adventure! We played several games of hide and seek, one of which involved Trinity crawling in the furnace closet, crouching against the furnace. Not exactly safe. Good thing I didn't know about it until the game was over. It was fun, though, and I know that for both the girls, this was a time to forget about everything and enjoy a totally kid-filled moment. It was for me, too.

After our hide and seek adventures, we shared lemonade and chocolate chip cookies on the back porch. Sitting in my white porch rocker, Trinity chatted a mile-a minute while nervously and savagely rocking. This wasn't the Trinity of a year and a half ago, I thought. The innocence and the hope seemed to have left her, leaving in its place world-worn burdens and a new knowledge of her place in it.

"My Mom's having a baby," she said, staring at the floor.

"Are you excited to have a new brother or sister?" I said, smiling and looking directly at her.

"No," she said. "If it is a girl, she'll be a skank like my sister. And if it is a boy, he'll get expelled from school like my brother did. I don't want to have any babies in our house."

"I'll bet your Dad is happy, right?" I said desperately looking for something positive to say.

"He isn't my Dad. It's Larry, my Mom's boyfriend. I wish my Mom wouldn't have boyfriends. Every time she has a boyfriend, there's a baby."

I glanced at Jasmine. Unusually quiet, she was fidgeting with her hair and staring out at my garden. "Well," I said, "I'm sure Larry is happy about the baby."

"I dunno," she said. "He's gone a lot."

Not quite knowing what to say now about this, I said, "Hey, do you want to go walk in the garden with Molly and Pickle?" Molly, of course, was my 20-year-old Siamese cat, and Pickle was my black rescue kitty, my soul-mate from a home in the Colorado mountains. Happy to be outside, I'm sure, the girls petted Molly and Pickle as they walked in the garden, touching and smelling the blooming flowers.

"K," Trinity said finally. "We have to go." As I walked with them to the front yard, I said, "It was good to see you both. I had fun." Righting their electric bikes, they were gone in a battery-powered instant.

Other than our few encounters, I knew nothing about Trinity, or Jasmine for that matter. Living in a small, close Southern community, it wasn't difficult to find out more about both of them.

Trinity was the third child in a soon-to-be four child family. Her mother was a nurse at the local hospital, and seemingly as good a mother as she could be under the circumstances. Trinity was right. Every time there was a boyfriend, there was a new baby. While she did receive some monetary help from the children's fathers, it wasn't quite enough to care for three and soon-to -be four children. So, to make ends meet, she picked up extra shifts at the hospital, leaving Trinity in the care of her eighteen-year-old brother and sixteen-year-old sister.

As the youngest child in the family so far, they teased and tormented her, as older siblings sometimes do, and so, Trinity would escape to the solace of her electric bike, aimlessly riding the streets of the neighborhood. In the weeks that followed our visit, I would see her, alone, standing by the retention pond, throwing stones into it and watching for the large turtles who lived there. She was sullen. The sparkle and innocence I once saw was gone, or deeply buried.

Jasmine was the oldest child in a two-child family. Being black in an all -white Southern community was difficult. Often, I would see her riding her electric bike with her three -year-old brother riding on the back. No helmets. I would hold my breath when I saw them, fearful that her brother would crash to the pavement as she raced through the neighborhood searching for freedom. The neighborhood kids, of course, teased her and made her sad. No wonder, I thought, she and Trinity became friends. I was happy that they had each other.

Over the next months, Trinity came to visit me often. Now leery about her sullen and anger-ridden state, and knowing about the potentials of a troubled child, I no longer invited her into my house. Instead, we always visited on my front porch or in my yard. I hated that I felt the need to do this, but I did have to protect myself.

Still, our visits were enjoyable. On one visit, we talked about school and the "new math". Totally clueless, Trinity taught me how to solve math problems "the new way" by lining up rocks on the sidewalk from my landscaping. I was proud of both of us. She was a good teacher, and I was an apt student.

"Hey," I said on that visit, "did you tell your Mom that I wrote a story about you?" "No," she said, playing with the rocks on the sidewalk. "Why not?" I asked. "Cause, I don't want her to know that I am going to be famous." "Oh. Ok," I said, deciding it was time to change the subject altogether.

On another visit, Trinity was picking up the glass pieces in my front garden landscaping. It was Christmastime, and I had sprinkled glass pieces among my white rock and sea shells that bordered my Southern plants. "You aren't going to steal those, are you?" I said. Seeing the hurt look in her eyes, I felt like a complete jerk for having said that, but she was different now, and I wasn't sure. In the minutes that followed, she took some of the green glass pieces that were shaped like Christmas trees and lined them in a row on the sidewalk. Next, she took the white pieces shaped like stars and put them above the trees. The resulting project was a beautiful Christmas scene. Somewhere in there, I thought, was the same girl I had originally met. I was suddenly sorry I had doubted that.

On one sunny and beautiful blue-sky Alabama afternoon, I was planting flowers on the side of my house. I loved doing this. Spring and summertime planting always made me happy. Suddenly, I heard a familiar sound. Trinity's electric bike! Ditching it on its side in my front yard, she approached me. "Whatcha doin'? she said. "I'm planting flowers along the side here." "Can I help?" she said. "Sure," I said, grateful for the company. Now as history with Trinity has taught me, I had no illusions that my flowers would be carefully spaced and planted. That was ok. I was glad to share this with her.

Grabbing an extra trowel, Trinity's planting skills were as I expected. Half dug in, they were a mis-match of distances, and the time to plant was a third of what I would have expected from myself. No matter. Seeing the look of happiness on her face was well worth it. She was, for once lately, completely happy. Taking my watering can to fill at the spigot, she danced happily along the driveway, crazily swinging the can above her head. She was again a carefree seven-year-old, innocent and full of hope. I smiled for her.

After our project was completed, I said, "I have four marigold plants left over. Would you like them?" "Really?" she said. "Sure!" So, we packed them on the rack in back of her bike, and off she went, driving at the battery speed of life.

I received an email message from Trinity's former teacher, Ms. Crutcher. Among other things, she said, "Thank you so much for taking the time to write me a letter and writing the story about Trinity. I was so moved by your thoughtfulness, it brought tears to my eyes. It reassured me that I am here for a reason and makes all the difficult days' worth it." Looks like this was a win for all of us.

In the coming months, it became increasingly clear that my housemate and best friend had the early stages of Alzheimer's. I loved my house and gardens, loved Fairhope, and loved the Gulf beaches, but I knew I needed to move back to Colorado to be with family.

When we listed the house and put the For-Sale sign in the yard, I wondered what Trinity would think. After a week, she drove her electric bike to my house and rang the doorbell. "Hi," I said. "How are you?" "What's that sign?" she said, clearly upset by it. "Well, sweetie, I have to move back to Colorado. I don't want to, but I have to." "Oh," she said, adopting her protective, defensive posture. "Ok. My flowers are growing in my bedroom. K. Thanks." And she was off.

After the sold sign was put up, I saw Trinity one more time. She rang the doorbell, and we met outside on the porch. She hugged me hard and said, "I'll miss you."

The story that was to make her famous was never published. It had too many words for the inclusion criteria in the contest, and I chose not to eliminate anything for fear it would compromise the integrity of the story.

Along life's journey, we have so many opportunities to learn from the people around us. Some are colleagues; some are neighbors; some are close friends; and some are innocent children navigating the obstacles on their own path. Trinity and I met at a time when we were both struggling to find our way. Though generations separated us, we were walking parallel paths that intersected at one critical point in time. The significance of Trinity's name was not lost on me. It was the symbol of hope, of struggle, and, finally, of acceptance.

Feeling life's discontentment, I once thought I needed to move across the country to start over and re-invent myself, and then, I remembered a performer at a concert I once attended who said, "Wherever you go, when you get there, that's where you'll be".

There is no re-invention, I realized—just moving forward. And you can do that from anywhere. I hoped Trinity moved forward, too, and found the desperately needed acceptance of herself. I think of her often and our brief journey together.

She is and always will be famous to me.

The Imposter

It was through a series of serendipitous events that I became a teacher. My senior year in college, I took a number of education classes required for people who wanted to become state certified teachers. I had no interest in either teaching or certification. I only took the classes because my mother insisted that I have "something to fall back on" in case I was not capable of a real career. She was, although she had no idea who he was, of the George Bernard Shaw philosophy, "He who can, does; he who cannot, teaches".

Some people know what their career path, their passion, is when they are six years old. They own it, pursue it, and achieve it. No drifting. I envied those people. I often thought, who does that as a young child?

I wasn't one of them. I had interests and skills, but no pre-destined drive to pursue a particular dream. When I graduated from college, I thought I would look for a job in the publishing industry. I had a Language Arts/Psychology degree and an interest in writing.

In 1970, job hunting meant dressing up, carrying a very thin resume, and putting feet to the streets cold-calling. I hated everything about it, except maybe the dressing up part. I just wasn't a cold-calling kind of girl.

While I was in the middle of this torture, I got a call from my brother, who was what I would call a success story in his own right. A delinquent by definition, he ditched school, built CO_2 rockets in the basement, and on one occasion blew up the neighbor's trash can, igniting the bushes, and nearly burning down their house. He was told by his high school guidance counselor to drop out of school because he would never amount to anything anyway. Ever the rebel, he chose not to drop out of high school, and, to further thumb his nose at the counselor's dire predictions, chose to apply to college.

Obviously not a scholar, he applied to a Presbyterian college in Kansas that would accept him on academic probation. Not surprisingly, he majored in biology. The only thing that ignited his passion as much as blowing up the neighborhood with CO_2 powered rockets was all species of bugs and insects. Not only did he get himself removed from academic probation, he went on to graduate with both bachelor's and master's degrees in biology. Just out of college, he applied to, interviewed for, and was hired for his first (and as it turns out, only) teaching job, one he held for thirty-three years until he retired.

During the first month of his first year, there was a teacher's strike at Bradley High School. Members of the teacher's union walked off the job in a dispute with the school board over salaries. Since classes were in session, the search was on to quickly find people stupid enough to cross a picket line to fill those positions. Hence, the call from my brother. I didn't want to teach. At 22, I didn't feel old enough or trained enough to teach high school students. Still, that kind of torture outweighed the torture of pounding the streets looking for work. So, I said yes.

At that age, I had no idea what it meant, either morally or physically to cross a picket line. The moral part I didn't get until a number of years later, but the physical part I found out on my first day. When I arrived, police cars were parked along the street. In front of the school entrance stretched a picket line of teachers standing shoulder to shoulder, blocking us from entering the school. They called us scabs and other things I can't mention here. Already anxious and feeling like an imposter because I didn't yet have a teaching certificate, I didn't know quite what to do. I was blocked and pushed and insulted in ways for which I was unprepared. Maybe aimlessly cold-calling hadn't been such a bad plan after all. Finally, a police officer escorted us "scabs" through the picket line and into the school.

A few days before my official first day of classes, I met with the English Department Chairman, Mabel Dankers. Four foot seven and round, she was old-school from her gray, curly hairdo right down to her old lady, chunky lace-up shoes. She was prim and pinched. When she saw my engagement ring, as part of the pre-interview small talk, she said, "Whom are you marrying"? Now I know the correct use of who and whom, but I would never say, "Whom are you marrying?" to anyone. Ever.

She talked of grammar, syntax, the importance of diagramming sentences, and all of the boring stuff that traditional English classes were made of. (See, I shouldn't have ended that sentence with a preposition, but I did anyway. Ah, ever the rebel!) I was sure this interview was going to be a disaster, and actually wouldn't have minded if it had been. Apparently, there was something about my young face and liberal attitude that she found somewhat endearing. I was smart, and, probably most importantly, I was a warm body to cover some of those abandoned classes. She hired me.

During the thirty-five-mile drive to Bradley High School on my first day of classes, I had plenty of time to think. What on earth was I thinking when I agreed to this?? I wasn't a teacher, didn't want to be a teacher, and, oh by the way, did I tell you that I had a fear of public speaking? I was about to teach high school seniors who were just four years younger than me. I tried not to let panic overwhelm me, but how could I possibly pull this off? I properly hyperventilated for thirty miles of the thirty-five-mile drive. At mile thirty, I dug deep and said, yes, you can do this, and steeled myself for what was to come.

The first few weeks, I didn't have to worry about lesson plans. They had already been done by the previous teacher. Boring, but done. My biggest challenge that day (besides crossing a picket line) was to create a presence. I was, in my own mind, an imposter in a real teacher's world, and a young imposter at that. I had to figure out how to relate to these kids. Act too young, and they would walk all over me. Reveal a hint of insecurity, and I would be a joke. Act too stern, and I would be a young B**** with an attitude. What to do...

When I greeted the first class, I thought of Rose and me. Together, what would we have done? Obviously, she wasn't with me, but she was in spirit. In a manner of speaking, we bowed to the audience and once again delivered a flawless performance. I was confident, poised, and had just enough of a sense of humor to win them over, and each class throughout the day got better and better. Not so bad after all.

I was an unconventional teacher, which I am sure is not surprising. I thought of my own experiences in English classes. Diagramming sentences with discipline and structure (an exercise I found to be largely a waste of everyone's time); unrelenting focus on punctuation exercises, bland

and rote; endless drills on verbs and verb tenses. If I suffered through those kinds of classes, I certainly wasn't about to let my students suffer in the same way.

After the first week, I ditched the existing lesson plans and thought long and hard about what I wanted the classroom experience to be. In 1970, there were no State-mandated objectives to be met, no "teaching to the standardized test" mentality. Certainly, there were departmental guidelines that bore the distinctive stamp of Mabel Dankers, but there was no State God of what and how to teach booming from the heavens. Teaching was a creative art, and I was determined to bring my own creative spirit to it.

English classes (as they were called in the 70's) were, in my mind, a wonderful blank canvas, unlike what a teacher might have in other disciplines, like math or history. They offered the opportunity to paint the human condition through literature, poetry, and writing. Focusing frantically on grammar, syntax, and punctuation would be like focusing on the chemical composition of the color blue. When you paint with the color blue, you quickly learn that blue is best used to illustrate water and skies, but doesn't really work to illustrate people's faces, unless, of course, you are painting Smurfs. Command of the English language comes through using it and studying the techniques that other classic writers used to create memorable pictures. My role was to be the master painter guiding them.

So, all things grammar and spelling were learned, not surprisingly, through writing. Journal keeping was mandatory, daily entries required, and journals were turned in to me weekly. Like true artists, they weren't told what to paint, only to paint and paint often. Every Friday, I collected 150 journals and commented on every single entry before Monday. Comments were written in purple ink. No red pens in my possession, ever. All tests were essay exams. Multiple-choice tests did not exist in my classroom. For students not skilled or confident in their writing ability, this was tough at first. Over time, they learned that I was a gentle critic, an artist leading them across the canvas of clear and accurate self-expression.

Poetry was taught, not just by reading the works of classic poets, but by analyzing the lyrics of contemporary song writers. The literature we shared together was chosen on the basis of its universal message, artistry, and impact.

My students repeatedly told me that for the first time they actually liked coming to English class. The secret wasn't in my teaching skills, although over time, I became quite skilled. The secret was that for fifty minutes a day we shared each other. It mattered to me that their time spent with me was meaningful and mutual.

Mabel Dankers, on the other hand, was not so pleased. Although my performance reviews by the Principal were very good, Mabel was not a fan of my teaching style. Inevitably, she called me into her office. She said, "You are young and inexperienced. You are not yet fully licensed by the State, although you have a provisional teaching certificate. We have departmental guidelines that I have drafted, and you are clearly sidestepping them. You need to focus on grammar exercises, and need to establish a formalized program for punctuation and spelling skills. This poetry teaching through song lyrics is unacceptable. I fully expect you will correct these deficiencies."

The Porter of today is very different from the Porter of the '70's. After Mabel expressed her clear displeasure, I cried, and cried hard.

By chance, Mary Jo, a fellow teacher who had been at BBHS for more than five years, stopped by my room and saw that I was clearly upset. She asked me what was going on. Reluctantly, I told her about my meeting with Mabel. She laughed and said, "Oh, Mabel. The most intellectual thing she has ever read in her lifetime is a story from the Reader's Digest. Don't worry about her. I, like you, want our kids to have meaningful experiences. Keep doing what you are doing. The kids love it, and they are learning from you."

For the next two years, I continued to teach my classes in the same way I had before being chastised by Mabel. As an affirmation that my teaching style was on the right track, I continued to get excellent performance reviews from the Principal, despite Mabel's objections.

Mabel was set to retire from teaching at the end of my second year at BBHS. A month before she left, she called me into her office. I went to see her with trepidation, of course. She said, "For two years, you have continued to ignore departmental guidelines. You have used methods and materials in your classroom that I would never have used, nor would I have encouraged you to use. Having said that, it has become clear to me that your students enjoy your classes and, most importantly, have learned a great deal from you. Though you are provisionally licensed, you seem to have become quite a good teacher, albeit, unconventional. I just wanted to tell you that before I left." There was a slight softening in Mabel's face as she told me this, although she was still pinched and prim.

What a backhanded compliment. I was good, but I wasn't a real teacher. An imposter, but one she apparently admired.

My two years at Bradley high School were an interesting introduction to the world of teaching. I grew a great deal as a person during those two years, not because of what I taught the kids, but because of what they taught me. Much to my surprise, I didn't like teaching. I loved it.

In 1972, two years after I had been a full-time teacher, I had to complete my student teaching in order to be fully licensed by the State of Illinois. Student teaching assignments were not a matter of choice, but of availability.

As luck would have it, my student teaching assignment was to teach a six-week class in rhetoric to high school juniors. My supervising teacher was a young version of Mabel Dankers. She was only slightly taller than Mabel, had curly brown hair (a bad perm, I think), and was twice as round. And, to round things out, so to speak, she was a control freak. Why are grammarians always short and round? There must be some correlation between the number of sentences diagramed and the number of doughnuts eaten. I am still thinking about that one.

For me, that summer student teaching experience was like jamming my size 9 foot into a size 8 shoe. It pinched and hurt. I could hardly imagine a worse experience for both me and the kids than teaching and learning rhetoric on beautiful summer days.

I didn't develop blisters that summer, because I was tired of being an imposter. Once and for all, I was going to be the real deal. I parked my creativity at the curb, did what she told me, and suffered through one of the worst summers of my life.

By August, teaching certificate in hand, I was no longer an imposter. A fully certified classroom artist, I was never to become a grammarian. I remained tall and thin. No diagramming sentences.

No doughnuts.

My Boys

In the teaching world, it is common knowledge that if you are a first-year teacher or a teacher new to a particular school, you don't get to choose the classes you are going to teach. On the contrary, the "newbies" get assigned to the schedules and classes none of the veteran teachers want. It is sort of like an unspoken hazing ritual.

Such was the case for me when I got a full-time teaching position at Hubbard Trail Middle School. Though I had been a teacher for three years in a different district, I was, it seemed, given the worst schedule and the worst classes possible that first year. My planning period was from 8 to 9; I taught one class before my assigned lunch at 10 in the morning; and for the rest of the day I had back-to-back classes until 3:30. No break.

Hubbard Trail was a 7th through 9th grade middle school, and my first year there, I taught all 8th grade classes. Students were ranked A through D based on academic performance, with the A level classes consisting of gifted students and the D level students reflecting the lowest student academic achievement level. The veteran teachers dubbed the D level students "the dumb and delinquent". Nobody wanted to teach them. Nobody. My classes that year consisted of four C level classes and one D level class.

As I looked over my class schedule, I realized that what I thought would be my biggest problem class, my D level class, was going to be a split class. Lasting from 11 to 12:30, their lunch break occurred in the middle of it. We had class from 11 to 11:30, lunch from 11:30 to 12:00, and the class resumed from 12:00 to 12:30. The worst students, as I thought, would have lunch in the middle of my class. Could this get any worse? How was I ever going to teach them anything??

The week before the students came back to school was an orientation and in-service week for teachers. During that week, I got acquainted with all of the staff, including the teachers in the Language Arts department. We met as a department and talked of classes, schedules, and students. The Language Arts teachers who taught the 7th grade students were particularly eager to share their stories and experiences with me when they learned which students would be in my 8th grade D level class.

"Oh, I can tell you stories about him! You've got your work cut out for you!"

"You'll never teach this kid anything. All he ever does is slouch into the room and go to sleep."

"You've got Eddie? You poor thing! Do you want me to tell you what to expect? He causes trouble all the time. He is unteachable and spends most of his time in the Assistant Principal's office."

As was always the case with me, I didn't want to know anything about previous history with any of the kids, especially the "dumb and delinquent". I wanted to form my own impressions based on our interactions together. I nicely told my colleagues this. "Ok," they said, "but forewarned is forearmed."

I can't say I wasn't worried about this D level class. I was. A lot.

On the first day of the first week of student classes, it was time for my 11:00 class to arrive. In they came, such as they were. They didn't file in or walk in; they barged in. Pumping and surging from their hormone and anger-filled bodies, they each came in the room differently. Some came in shuffling with attitude, taking a seat, and putting their heads down to sleep. Some came in punching their friends and fighting over which seat to take. Some plopped down, putting their feet on top of the desk, glaring at me. And some came in beaten down, expecting more of the same of what they were used to. It was, it turns out, a class of all boys.

Not a single girl.

20 of them.

When the bell rang, it was show time. This day would be the most important for me, for them, and for our year long relationship together.

There is a psychological term in some circles for objects between people which block the energy flow. Furniture—desks, podiums, coffee tables, long tables. Sunglasses. Fences. I don't like constructs, ever, in any situation, but particularly when I am trying to form a bond between myself and 20 defensive boys. So, on this first day of class, I didn't sit behind my desk or stand behind the podium. I sat on the edge of my desk, swinging my legs.

The leg swinging was an intentional action. As a trained counselor as well as teacher, I was aware of certain techniques that psychologically would help me bond with these kids, and God knows, I needed all the help I could get. The leg swinging was a technique called body language mirroring. It is an unspoken way of saying, "I am like you. I feel the same." These boys came into the room wiggling, punching, and posturing, their way of saying, "I'm uncomfortable being here." My leg swinging said, "I'm slightly uncomfortable, too. We have something in common."

While they wiggled, squirmed, and casually punched each other, I said, "I'm Mrs. Penn. Over the next school year, we will be sharing 8th grade Language Arts together, something I am sure you aren't too crazy about. During the next few days, I will be telling you my expectations and hopes for this class. Equally important are your expectations for me."

"I want you to do me a favor now. I want you to take out a piece of paper, put your name on it, and tell me something you think I should know about you. It can be things you like, things you don't like, feelings you have about being here. It can be anything. I don't care what you say. It's your choice. Just say something. I don't care if you think you aren't any good at writing or spelling at this point. Just write what you think I should know about you. At the end of class, I want you to drop your papers in this box on my desk. Not doing it is not an option. I'll give you ten minutes to do this for me."

With much groaning and resistance, they took out paper reluctantly and started writing, clearly annoyed that they had to do anything except listen to me talk, or best case, sleep.

This time gave me the chance to observe them. Still sitting on the edge of my desk, I had a clear view of this emotionally disheveled bunch. Dressed in jeans, plaid shirts or t-shirts, they looked like every other 8th grader in the building. But it was the attitude that impacted me the most. Aside from the typical adolescent hormone surging, there was something else. They each seemed to carry an emotional backpack filled with hurt, disappointment, and rejection. And, I had no doubt they would swing it at you if you exposed their hidden truths.

While I was in the midst of this classroom observation, a hand in the back of the room shot up. "Eddie," I said, "what do you need?" Aside from having a very good memory, I made it a priority to learn the names of my students on the first day. It sent the message that it mattered to me to be able to match a face with a name.

"I can't do this. I don't have any paper," Eddie said.

"Lucky for you, I have a lot of paper and will gladly give you some." I got down from the desk, grabbed a piece of paper, walked to the back of the room, and handed it to Eddie. "Here you go," I said. "You're all set." Eddie grabbed the paper out of my hand and slouched in the chair. For five of the ten minutes, he did nothing. Finally, he angrily began to write.

This first class with my boys was pretty much what I expected it to be. Departure and return from lunch were completely chaotic. As for my rapport building that first day, I'd give myself a C minus. But every boy dropped a paper of things I should know about them in my inbox. I would guess it was because I said that not doing it wasn't an option.

I took their papers home with me that night, not only because I was curious, but because that was my way. If I asked them to do something for me, I had to do something for them. Their responses were intense and surprisingly candid.

"My old man hates me. You'll probably hate me, too. I don't care."

"I'm only in this stupid class because I have to be."

"What good is it to learn to spell? I'm never going to right anything anyway."

"All you teachers do is tell us what we do wrong. You all think we are dumb."

"Nobody cares enough about us to give us books like everybody else gets. Why should we bother to write this shit anyway?"

I can't quite describe how I felt when I read these papers. I guess the best I can say is that I hurt for them. The last one from Eddie troubled me. I didn't know what he meant about not having books.

The next day, my boys came in to the classroom as expected. They punched and sulked and skulked in, but there was a new activity. Two of the boys barged in and knocked each other to the floor. The dominant boy straddled the weaker boy, took his fingers, and began to pull at the weaker boy's eyebrows. I learned later this was called eyebrow assault.

Adolescent boys, particularly troubled boys, have a great need to touch and be touched. They do. But they don't want to be perceived as gay or "funny". So, they punch each other, knock each other down, and do strange things like eyebrow assault. I knew this, so, ok, fine. I just let them do what they needed to do until the bell rang.

When it was time for class to start on this second day together, I said," Hey, get out your grammar, spelling, and literature books." My request resulted in mixed reactions. Some boys looked at me like I was clueless. Some sulked. And, Eddie, my Eddie, spoke up. "We don't get no books."

"What do you mean you don't have books? Did you leave them in your locker?"

Angrily, Eddie said, "Don't you get it? We don't get books."

"What do you mean you don't get books?" I said. "Didn't you get them checked out to you in homeroom? That's where everybody gets their books checked out to them for the year. "

"Not us," Eddie said. "Everybody is afraid we will just rip them up or throw them away, so we don't get books." Heads nodded in agreement with Eddie.

Stunned because I was new to this school district, I said," I don't understand this. I believe you, but I am going to find out why you don't get books." The rest of the class that day was seat-of-your-pants fill-in. While I did ok, I would give myself a D for content. To my credit, at least nobody was asleep.

At the end of the next day, I went down to the Principal's office. Joe Crawford was an interesting guy. With a Doctorate in Education, he was the least likely guy you would see in a middle school. But, keep in mind, this was the 70's. Joe had a ponytail and rode a motorcycle to school, not exactly the image of a middle school Principal by today's standards. But he was smart, good at his job, and equally important, the kids respected him. A troubled boy himself in middle school, Joe had committed almost every delinquent act possible, and so, as Principal, he was always ten steps ahead in anticipating when trouble was about to happen. It was like one street kid sizing up another.

"So, Joe," I said, "I have a D level class I am concerned about. They said they don't get books checked out to them, and I was wondering why."

"Yeah, no they don't. I know you are new here, Penn, so I will tell you why they don't. The school board has ruled that we can't sustain the losses from their delinquency. It's too costly. They believe that if we assign books to these kids, they will just destroy them. The school board believes that if they have access to books in the classroom under supervision, they will get what they need. They believe that there is no need to check books out to them."

I was silent for a minute and then responded. "I understand financial loss and that you would be accountable for these losses. I really do get it. What I don't get is that we're making assumptions about behavior that hasn't even occurred. Worse, the message we are sending to these D level students and everybody else in this building is that if you are academically or socially challenged, you are automatically trouble. During the last couple of days, the boys in my D level class said everybody knows they are in the "dumb classes" because they don't carry books in the hall and don't have books in their lockers. They said it is like having a sign on your head that says, "Here comes Stupid". They told me it makes them angry. I don't know how you would feel, but it would make me angry, too, and sad. So, I will make you a deal. Let me check out books to these kids for the year. If they tear them up, I'll pay for them. They just want to be like everybody else, and I want that for them, too."

Joe hesitated for a couple of minutes and then said, "Ok, Penn, here's what I'll do. I'll contact the board members about your request. I'll back you up, but you are on the hook for this. It probably will cost you."

When my boys came to class on Friday, books were stacked on my desk. Since there was no room for me to sit on my desk as usual, I stood beside it as the raucous entry began. After the punching, pushing, and eyebrow assault stopped and the bell rang, they sat down in their now customary fashion.

"So, you guys," I said, "these are your books. You can carry them in the hall, put them in your lockers, or take them home if you want. They are yours for the year. I only have two things I'd like you to do for me. Bring them to class every day, and take care of them. I'd like to be able to pass them on to next year's class."

If there is one moment in time that I remember about this class after all these years, it was this moment. There was a stunned silence. The wiggling stopped; the posturing stopped. It was quiet. Nobody gets excited about having grammar, spelling, and literature textbooks, especially kids who fear their contents. But they were. They weren't excited about the books. They were excited about what having books meant. They were like everybody else now! Even I underestimated the impact this would have.

On Monday when they returned to class, my boys seemed to be a little less raucous when they entered. Yes, they punched each other and eyebrow assaulted, but it seemed slightly less intense. And they stopped well before the bell rang.

Sitting on my desk, swinging my legs, I looked out over the class. Neatly stacked on their desks were all of their books. Every single boy brought his books to class. Every one of them. Ah ha, I thought, it's a start.

Though classified as 8th graders, my boys' skill sets varied. Most of them, as I learned, had reading skills at the 6th grade level or below, and their spelling skills were well below that. In the 70's, there were no national or state mandated standardized tests to teach to. While there were annual assessment tests throughout the school, teaching was still a creative art. This class was a blank canvas. What should we paint and how should we paint it?

There were two things I already knew I needed to do right away. Since my boys were not conventional in any sense of the word, I couldn't imagine that a conventional classroom of seats in military style rows would work to accomplish all I needed to do here. The other thing I needed to do was to find a reading book that they could relate to—something a little less formal and intimidating than their reading textbooks. My goal was to get them to read, to want to read, and to enjoy reading together as a class. No intimidation. No embarrassment.

First things first. The classroom seating structure.

"Ok, guys. Here's what I want you to do. I want you to move your desks anywhere in the room that you would like them to be. Just move them. Ideally, I'd like you to move them close to your friends, but if you would rather be alone for now, I'm fine with that. I only have one request—no rows."

At this, even the slouchers and the desperately defiant sat up.

"What?" they said.

"I said I would like you to move your desks anywhere in the room that you would like them to be—but no rows."

The desk moving took the first half hour before the break for lunch. It resulted in quite a pattern. Actually, there was no pattern. Some desks formed a circle, some desks faced each other, no doubt for ease of punching and eyebrow assaulting, and some were dragged as far to the back of the room as possible and to the farthest corner away from everyone. Eddie's desk was among those in the very back.

After the raucous return from lunch, everyone went to their carefully placed desks. I still sat on the edge of my desk, but I was no longer swinging my legs. My message— I'm not uncomfortable anymore, either. The downside to this creative endeavor was that the class that followed my boys had a different personality and different needs. They thrived on order and routine. So, every day during the 10-minute passing period between classes, I had to move all of the desks back to military rows. It was ok. It was worth it.

In the next few days, I found a supplementary reading book that I thought would capture my boys' attention. Though written at a 6th grade reading level, it presented as a book any adult would pick up and read. It was a book of interesting trivia for the curious. Among other things, my boys certainly were curious. I thought they would like this book, so I bought 20 of them and one for myself.

During the next months and weeks in this crazily arranged classroom, together we tackled academic areas that previously brought about fear and defensive behaviors. Sometimes, I sat on the edge of my desk, but many times I sat in a student desk among them. I first time I did this, I could feel their tension. I was invading their safe space. But once they learned I wasn't critical or judgmental and wouldn't hurt them, they relaxed and were more comfortable with me sitting next to them.

Spelling was a challenge for my boys. We used their traditional spelling books, and I tried my best to teach them to use mental cues to help them remember how certain words were spelled. The months of the year were problematic, as were the days of the week, both important spelling skills for everyday life. As for the days of the week, Saturday seemed to be a stumbling block for them. Why Saturday, I'm not sure. They learned to spell Wednesday and Thursday using the cues I taught them, but Saturday was still a problem for them.

So, one day, I wrote the word Saturday on the chalkboard. I wrote Sa-TURD-ay. "Look at this word," I said. "Look carefully. What's in the middle of it?"

Eddie blurted out, "Oh man, that says turd!!" "Indeed, it does," I said. "Now remember that when you spell the word." Unconventional, yes. Did it work? Yes. All my boys now learned to spell the word Saturday. I often wonder if they still think of this when they see the word Saturday.

In reading, we used their assigned textbooks, but their favorite book was the book of trivia. They learned how the ice cream cone came to be, the history of denim jeans, and about the creator of the sandwich. But most importantly, they read. They read because they were interested; they read because they loved the stories; and they read because we were together.

An interesting thing happened over time. Their classroom entrance was calmer. They came in less aggressive or sullen and went to their desks well before the bell rang. No one slept, ever. Dismissal to lunch was smoother and, on most days, they returned more calmly well before the bell rang. And the desks. The desks that were in the far corners of the back of the room slowly moved to the center. They felt safe now, and I was among them every day in a student desk.

My boys were not only academically challenged, they were socially challenged, too. Most of them, but not all of them, came from low income families who couldn't afford school lunches. Though they had low income assistance in the form of free lunch punch cards, they didn't want to use them. If they used their cards, everybody knew they were poor, and they didn't want that. So many days, they went without lunch. They said they weren't hungry, but I knew better.

And so, I told my boys, "Hey, I know some days you forget your lunch money. I get that. Sometimes, I forget mine, too. So now, I have a money box in the back of the room. If you forget your money and you're hungry, just take money out of the money box for lunch. If you can put the money back later for the next guy, great. If not, there's still money in the box for you to use when you need it." Sometimes as they could, they put money back in the box. Most times, though, I replenished it. But never did anyone steal from it. Ever.

In February of that year, I was pregnant with my first child and was slightly showing. I decided to share this news with my classes. When I shared with my boys, their reaction was predictable. They were quiet, but wiggling. Imagining that your teacher ever had sex, as teenage boys would do on hearing the news of my pregnancy, was disconcerting for them. But something else happened. They became very, very protective.

One day when I came in to their 11 o'clock class, a comfortable high-backed chair was sitting in the middle of the room. After they sat down in their desks and the bell rang, I said, "Wow, where did this chair come from?" Eddie, my Eddie, always the spokesperson for the class, who by the way DID learn that year and never went to the Assistant Principal's office from my class, said, "Now, Mrs. Penn, don't ask where this chair came from. We just want you to be comfortable. Sitting on your desk isn't good for you, and sitting in one of our desks isn't either."

"Thank you, boys. That was really sweet." Though wondering where it came from, I sat in it and enjoyed the comfort that day. Of course, I knew this chair came from somewhere. After considerable investigation, I went to the Assistant Principal's office.

"Al," I said, "I'm pretty sure the boys in my 11 o'clock class stole a chair out of your office. They didn't mean anything.

They were worried about me being pregnant and wanted me to be comfortable. I'll bring it back to your office."

Al sighed and looked at me. "Penn," he said, "Eddie Sanford and none of the other boys in your 11 o'clock class have been to my office all year. I don't know what you are doing in there with them, but if all of the teachers were like you, I'd likely be out of a job. Keep the chair. You've earned it."

And I did keep it. I sat in that chair for the rest of the school year. I was comfortable, and my boys were pleased.

In early May, school assessment tests were coming up. My boys were, of course, anxious and defensive about it. I said, "It's just a test. So what? Think about what you have learned this year, what we have learned together. I know you don't believe this right now, but you will be fine. I've seen how much you all have improved this year. I have great confidence in you."

When the scores of the assessment tests came in, my boys had improved two grade levels above where they were in the previous year, and their spelling and grammar skills were at the 8th grade level. All of them. My boys did it, as I knew they would.

As the end of the school year approached, we all felt an encroaching sadness. Next year they would move on to the ninth grade and a new teacher. "Just remember this," I told them. "We have had an extraordinary experience together, and you will again next year. Just believe in yourselves and you will do well. I'm so proud of all of you."

At the final bell on the last day of class together, every single boy gave me a hug. Eddie, my Eddie, ever the spokesperson for the class, was last. "We all love you, Mrs. Penn." They didn't love me. They loved that someone finally accepted them for who they were—trustworthy and capable.

As for paying for damage to their textbooks, there was nothing to pay for. Every book was returned. Not one was destroyed or damaged.

Pre-judging people is easy. Understanding, accepting, and appreciating people for who they are—for their uniqueness—is where the real work begins, but the work is well rewarded. My boys taught me that.

This 11 o'clock class that I had dreaded so much became an oasis in the day for all of us. For 50 minutes each day, the emotional backpacks of hurt, disappointment, and rejection were put aside. We could just be ourselves, share, and learn from each other. Of all the classes in my teaching career, this is the one I will never forget.

After all, they were—and always would be—my boys.

Boots Penn

L anguage Arts, like math, geography, or history, can be a challenging subject to teach to middle and high school students. Unless you get to teach gifted students who excel at, and like, almost everything, it's hard to keep the average adolescent fully engaged.

There are reasons for that. First of all, the subject matter can be tedious and dull, particularly if it pertains to grammar, punctuation, and spelling. But more importantly, the teenage mind feels that it is far better served by focusing on other more important stuff, like clothes, makeup, and who's hot and who's not. Now, *these* are the essential things they thought one should focus on.

During my second year of teaching at Hubbard Trail Middle school, I was the unwitting recipient of a Language Arts class I later came to call My Lip Gloss Class. Average academics, this class consisted of four boys and twenty-six girls. With the exception of the boys and three girl outliers, it seemed I was teaching the entire cheerleading squad in a single class. If you have ever seen the movie or read Amanda Brown's book Legally Blonde, it was like having twenty-three copies of Elle Woods, minus the academic acuity, sitting in my classroom. What on earth was I going to do with them?

As I looked out over this headshaking class, my eyes focused on the back of the room. Sitting in the last seat of the first row was a girl quite unlike the others. Her name was Tammy, quite a feminine name for a not so feminine girl. Leaning back in her desk with her legs sprawled out in front of her, she was a large, hulking girl, though not fat. Squinty-eyed, combative, and skeptical, her body language said if you say the wrong thing to me, I'm knocking you out. That was, of course, a defense against all the turmoil raging inside of her. Still, I knew I shouldn't push it until I got to know her better. Don't poke the bear until you have a darn good defense, I thought. As you can imagine, Tammy had nothing but distain for The Lip Gloss Girls, the Elle Woods lookalikes.

Ahh, The Lip Gloss Girls. After the first two weeks of class, their behavior became predictable. They came into class, mostly as a group, provocatively twitching and adjusting their clothes, no doubt hoping the four boys in the class were watching. Before the bell rang, and certainly well after, they spent considerable time applying lip gloss, ½ inch thick at a time, and smoothing their sticky lips repetitively. I kept thinking, I pitied the poor guy who kissed any of those lips. He wouldn't have been kissed; he would have been slimed.

They gossiped about the guys on the basketball team and football team, about the brands of glossy nail polish, which they secretly tried to apply in class, but were quickly outted by the smell, and which guys' butts looked good in their jeans. Really? How could I compete with the likes of that?

And there was the note passing. Folded with origami precision, these notes, so furtively passed, didn't escape my attention. Their contents a lifeline of importance among them, The Lip Gloss Girls spent the great majority of their class time penning them. I didn't stop them. I just secretly hoped that they were writing in complete sentences and that their spelling was accurate.

There were two other distinct behaviors these Lip Gloss Girls displayed. They were gum poppers and cheek biters, in the 70's a sure sign that you held high status in the popularity club. The gum of choice generally was Juicy Fruit, the aroma of which wafted through the classroom like some teenage aphrodisiac. The gum popping itself was an art. Popular girl popped their gum constantly, but not crudely. It could be heard, but it popped with a certain dental chic that branded them as clearly part of the in-crowd.

But the piece de resistance was the cheek biting, the clear symbol that you were all that and so much more! Popular girls would bite the inside skin of their cheeks, resulting in a slight twist to the mouth. It was the Lip Gloss symbol of confidence, popular allure, and solid membership in the top of the food chain social club.

Not a girly-girl myself (although I could be if the proper situation warranted it), I did manage to bond quickly with The Lip Gloss Girls on one level. My shoes. I always sat on the top of my desk with my legs hanging over, providing a clear view of my shoes. I have always had good taste in shoes and have had a great deal of shoe variety, mostly the most popular styles. Apparently, this fact was not lost on The Lip Gloss Girls, who frequently complimented me on my shoe choice. Well...sigh...at least we bonded on something.

And then there was Tammy. Clearly a very intelligent girl, she was, I believe, placed in average classes because she was rebellious and didn't care at all about annual school-wide testing, which was the basis for class placement. Most days in the early weeks of our class, she would roll her eyes out loud at The Lip Gloss Girls' antics and would put her head down on her desk so she wouldn't have to look at them. I can't say I blamed her. Though she would, reluctantly, complete her assignments from me, it was clear that she liked neither the assignments nor the Lip Gloss clique.

What could I do to save this class? It was boring, even for me. One night, as I was plowing through a stack of underwhelming punctuation assignments taken from the textbook, I glanced over at my cat Boots. Boots was a rescue cat with attitude. While she could be loving, it was always preceded by an icy eye showdown between us. Neither of us, of course, would back down until we both decided this was silly and a waste of time. Sometimes, I would approach her first. She would eyeball me, gloating as if she had won, but wouldn't run from me. She lovingly accepted all the pets and cuddling I gave her. Sometimes, she would just jump in my lap, clearly announcing that the showdown was over, on her terms, of course.

Glancing at her and reflecting on her attitude, I had an idea. What if I created a story about Boots and used the storyline to create sentences that we could use for grammar and punctuation exercises? The content could be entertaining as the kids learned the necessary, but dull, grammar and punctuation skills. It just might work. It was worth a try. The following weekend, I began to write the story of Boots Penn.

Particularly in the music business, there are popular singers known only by a single name. Madonna, Cher, Kesha, Pink, Ringo, Prince. Then there are other singers who have to be called by both names. Elton John, Billy Joel, Melissa Etheridge, Adam Levine, Garth Brooks, Lady Gaga. A single name just wouldn't cut it for them. Such was the case for the Boots character. She could never be called Boots.

She always had to be called Boots Penn.

As the Boots Penn story began to take shape, here are the basics. One evening, when I was grading papers and my husband was watching a basketball game, we heard a forceful, loud knock on the front door. It was insistent and repetitive. We both looked at each other and said, "Who can *that* be?" Together, we went to the front door and opened it.

Standing in front of us was Boots Penn. Sporting a red bandana on her head, she was dressed in a leather jacket, leather chaps, and wore heavy motorcycle boots. At 6'2, she was an imposing figure, but not fat. "Excuse me," she said. "I wonder if you could help me out. I coasted my motorcycle into your yard on fumes. I don't have enough gas to get to a gas station and wondered if I could stay the night with you until the morning when I can get to a gas station." Clearly stunned, my husband and I looked at each other, looked at her, and glanced at the Harley-Davidson motorcycle parked on our lawn.

"We don't generally let strangers into our house, and especially this late," I said. As I said this, I couldn't help but notice the beautiful black and white fur on her face and on her large hands.

With an icy stare but a sweet purring voice, she replied. "I am so sorry to bother you. I don't usually do this kind of thing either, but I really am in a jam and need some help. I promise I won't cause you any trouble, and I'll be gone in the morning."

I looked at my husband. She did seem sweet, didn't seem to belong to a motorcycle clowder, and with that icy stare and 6'2 frame towering above both of us, it was hard to say no. And so, she stayed.

And stayed.

And stayed.

Over the coming weeks and months, we learned a great deal about Boots Penn. Very sweet, but highly manipulative, Boots Penn was fiercely independent and had an extraordinary taste for expensive food. Not cat food. People food. She loved steak, lobster, shrimp, and crab legs. Ever the partier, she drank beer and smoked pot with her friends in our basement. She was, over time, so happy with her "arrangement" with us that she adopted our last name. Her name now was Boots Penn.

And so, the story unfolded. The first class to receive the Boots Penn story was, of course, The Lip Gloss Class. Written as a series of sentences requiring proper punctuation and grammar correction, the sentences told the story of Boots Penn's unanticipated arrival at our house, her lack of accepting any domestic responsibility, her passion for expensive food, and her perpetual partying.

After handing out this first Boots Penn assignment, I sat on my desk observing their reactions. A few minutes passed before several of The Lip Gloss Girls giggled. The boys, all four of them, had varying reactions. Tim had a quizzical look on his face as if to say, "What the heck is this?" Jason grinned. Tommy laughed as if he recognized a kindred spirit. Alex glanced from side to side saying out loud, "Really?" And Tammy, sprawled out in the back of the room, smirked. Though it was too early to tell, it seemed as though this story telling just might work.

Over the next several weeks, the Lip Gloss Class eagerly embraced the saga of Boots Penn. They actually looked forward to their assignments. Perhaps it was time to roll it out to my other classes.

And so, I did.

The rest, they say, is history. Each of my classes truly enjoyed the Boots Penn saga, and she became one of the many topics of hallway conversations. My husband was a math teacher at Hubbard Trail Middle school, and we shared many of the same students. After they would leave my class and would go to his class, they would bombard him with questions about Boots Penn. Was it true that you both had to get second jobs to afford her expensive taste in food? Did she get into an intoxication-fueled altercation with some of her friends, resulting in a significant scrape to her pink nose, but no loss of fur? Did she really trash your basement with her parties, expecting you to clean up after her, only to have pangs of conscience that ultimately made her help? Was she an outdoor grill meister who cooked outdoors on the weekends, wearing a chef's hat and an apron that said Kool Kat, emblazoned with a marijuana plant? Without rehearsal, Bob and I were synchronized on every Boots Penn adventure and detail. He never skipped a beat, nor did I.

After eight years of the continuing Boots Penn saga, Bob and I left Hubbard Trail and moved to Colorado. I could never quite tell if the kids were going to miss us or the on-going story of Boots Penn. She was legendary in the halls of Hubbard Trail and, so I heard, remained so for many years after we left.

The willing suspension of disbelief allows us to suspend logic, and briefly, allows us to believe in something surreal for the sake of enjoyment. This certainly was the case for the students' infatuation with the legendary Boots Penn. Boots Penn, of course, was the symbol of the teenage condition. She was fiercely independent and rebellious, but ultimately vulnerable and fragile. She was representative of the things they imagined doing, but never actually would do.

From time to time, we all need to go to a place in our minds that we know isn't real, but seems real, and brings us pleasure. It is a brief respite from our daily challenges and allows us to refuel and regenerate.

A year after my husband and I moved to Colorado and were walking on Boulder's Pearl Street mall, we encountered a young man who said, "Mr. and Mrs. Penn?" We looked quizzically at him, and then I said, "Chris, is that you?" "It is," he said. A junior at CU Boulder, he asked how we were, how the kids were doing, and what we were doing in Boulder. Without hesitation, he then asked about Boots Penn. At twenty-one years of age, he hadn't forgotten about the famous Boots Penn. Without skipping a beat, we both said that she still rode her motorcycle, had extravagant parties, and was loving the Colorado climate. And yes, we both had second jobs to afford her expensive taste in food. With that, Chris grinned as if being re-united with a long-lost friend.

The Lip Gloss Girls were never academic in the year I taught them. I wasn't quite sure that they ever would be, but I always held out hope that with the right inspiration, they would focus on other things besides the allure of teenage popularity.

As for Tammy, one Monday when she came to class, she stopped by my desk. Never one to approach, ever, she said in her typical surly and skeptical fashion, "I drove by your house this weekend with some friends of mine, and I didn't see no cat cookin'.

"Ahh," I said grinning in response, "but you looked."

This, of course, was the magic of the Boots Penn legacy, even, and especially, for a girl like Tammy.

My Menagerie

I am a self-confessed animal addict. I have had twenty-seven pets in my lifetime, not counting three guinea pigs, a rabbit, a mouse, and countless tropical fish.

My early experience with family pets, not being what I wanted for myself later in life, perhaps triggered my need to save as many of the animal souls looking for love and safety as I could. Feeling unlovable and unrooted for much of my life, I seemed to be drawn to the animal spirits who were sad, neglected, and scared, as I have been.

From the Drain, I remember every pet, their names, the reason I rescued them, and their unique needs and personalities. Like a video montage, special moments run through my mind and make me smile in remembrance.

My first dog after I left my childhood home was Penny. Newly-weds, my husband and I wanted an addition to our family. Together, we found a private owner whose dog recently had puppies. A Lab, Irish Wolfhound, German Pointer mix, Penny was hard to resist. She had the black Lab face and ears, the round puppy body, and the smell. The puppy smell! We were sold, and so was she—to us!! Everywhere we went with her, people were drawn to her, petted her, and loved her. What was not to love?

Ahh, Penny. She probably was compromised early on because we named her Penny Penn. Poor baby. Who does that to a dog? Smart, but stubborn, she grew into an adult dog who looked nothing like the Lab puppy we fell in love with. A strange mix, her cute Lab ears became the folded ears of a Wolfhound, and her temperament was, well, different. She was smart, loving, and sweet, but she danced to the beat of a different drummer. Clearly, she had her own crazy agenda. She was hard-headed and wild.

Penny's vet called her a nutty dog. I absolutely agreed with that.

At the age of two, she contracted heartworm disease. Living on a three-acre farm near the forest preserve in Northern Illinois, mosquitoes were prevalent. After a series of arsenic treatments in those days the prescribed treatment for dogs who contracted heartworm, the vet announced to us that she was the only dog he had ever seen who never got sick from the treatments. Ever. He said she acted as though she had just eaten a steak dinner. That was my Penny. Cast iron stomach and a very hard head.

Once, when we had guests over for dinner, I had just put the spaghetti dish I made on the table and turned my back to get the salad and bread, when I heard a sound. Glancing over my shoulder, I saw Penny rounding the corner, running full speed from the sun room into the dining room. She leaped full force, legs spread in the air, and landed on the dining room table. "No! Penny, no!" I said in anticipation of what was about to happen. Too late! Enticed by the seductive smell of spaghetti, she stuck her nose into the dish and snarfed the spaghetti down until she nearly lost her breath. Not only had she consumed most of our main course, spaghetti sauce and dog slobber were stuck to the tablecloth, the placemats, and the plates. Totally embarrassed, thanks to Penny, we went straight to Plan B that night. We ordered out! Our friends did come to dinner again after that, but I'm not sure why. Maybe they were intrigued by what Penny might do next to top what became affectionately known as The Spaghetti Incident.

Over the years, Penny became obsessed with eating things. On one afternoon, she completely devoured her nylon leash and ate more than half of my leather briefcase that was sitting on the floor beside the sofa. Included in the collateral damage were my students' homework assignments. Imagine how I felt when I had to announce to my students that *my* dog ate *their* homework! They thought it was funny. I, on the other hand, did not. Other than turning from black to a pale shade of grey that day, she managed to fully digest the leash and the briefcase, making a healthy deposit of both in our backyard. Cast iron stomach, indeed.

Next, Penny became obsessed with my refrigerator. Seeing me open and close it daily, she would eyeball the delectables inside. Intelligent, stubborn, and always thinking, she realized that if she stuck her nose into the gasket and pushed hard enough, the refrigerator riches were hers for the taking. And she took them. Often! On more than one occasion, I would come home from work to find the refrigerator door open and the bottom shelf completely cleaned out. The residuals, of course, were scattered on the kitchen floor, the dining room rug, and on the living room chairs and sofa.

Now, sometimes, dogs are smarter than humans. If I knew Penny had a great refrigerator talent, why would I continue to put things on the bottom shelf of the refrigerator? According to Albert Einstein, the definition of insanity is doing the same thing over and over again and expecting a different result. Clearly, by his definition, I was insane.

So, I came home from work one day to find the refrigerator door open—again—and an entire corned beef brisket gone!! Eaten!! Penny was cowering in the corner, clearly aware of her grave indiscretion. I was so angry, steam was shooting out of my ears! How could she? I had had plans for that corned beef! Despite my anger, I did feel sorry for nutty Penny, cowering and shaking in the corner. At least she had the good sense to have some remorse. In the end, I decided the best punishment for Penny was to take her water away for an hour or so to give her the chance to think about what she had done.

Tit for tat, sometime during the middle of the night, Penny responded by leaving me a healthy corned beef deposit on my dining room rug. That, of course, was my vindictive, nutty girl.

In the days that followed, my Einstein insanity definition abandoned, the refrigerator door was secured with rows and rows of duct tape. With no more refrigerator raids, Penny and I came to an understanding, at least on that front. The trash can contents, not so much. A new frontier, Penny directed her food obsession to the kitchen trash can now that she could no longer raid the refrigerator.

After we first got Penny, I was smart enough to know that dogs are often attracted to trash can contents, and so I bought a trash can with a lid that opened when you stepped on the pedal at the base. I was on this!! Ahh, never underestimate the skills of a very rebellious, intelligent, nutty dog. Apparently, over time, Penny observed my actions as I made multiple deposits in the trash can. Shortly after the refrigerator taping, I came home from work to find the trash can lid open and the trash can contents strewn though-out the house. Food contents were devoured and paper products shredded with passionate precision. My house was a paper nightmare.

How is this possible, I thought? The trash can has a lid that can only be opened by pressing the foot pedal at the base. After I cleaned up the mess, I thought about my nutty Penny. Smart and always the observer, she must have watched me hundreds of times make deposits in the trash can, calculating my measured movements.

On the weekend, after the trash can incident, my husband, Bob, was outside cutting the grass. Normally, I would be outside trimming and picking the wild weeds that grew near our forest preserve property. Today, while Penny was in the house feeling that she was alone, I hid quietly in the bedroom, waiting to see what she would do. After forty-five minutes, she made her move. Slightly cracking the bedroom door, I had a straight-line view of her antics. Stealthily, she approached the trash can. Lifting her left front paw and pushing down on the pedal, the trash can treasures were hers for the taking! Once again, nearly losing her breath, she proceeded to eat the food contents and shred all the remaining paper products. Ah ha! That's how she did it!!

Like the refrigerator door, the trash can later was secured with multiple rows of duct tape. I had Penny-proofed my kitchen. Or so I thought.

My kitchen had heavy, solid oak cabinets. While I kept most of my food items in the cabinets above the counter, I did keep my supplies for cookie making in one lower cabinet. A corner lazy-susan design, it took a good, solid push to swivel the shelf around. It should come as no surprise to anyone that I came home from work to find my entire kitchen covered with flour, sugar, and dog slobber. No longer able to raid the refrigerator or the trash can, she had set her sights on the lazy-susan contents. Penny, once a shiny black, was now a ghostly grey, her eye area and snout crystalized with sugar.

After this incident, my lazy-susan corner cabinet was secured with—you guessed it—duct tape. Though my kitchen now looked like the hillbilly version of This Old House, it was finally Penny-proofed. See, humans can learn, can't they?

My next pet acquisition was Boots. I was always a cat lover but hadn't had a cat since I was a kid. My teacher friend, Paula, approached me one day at work. She said that a friend of hers who owned a large farm found a litter of kittens on his property. A no-nonsense kind of guy, he had neither the time nor the inclination to keep these kittens, even as barn cats. He was going to get a sack and drown them in the river. Paula pleaded with him to give her 48 hours to find homes for them. Reluctantly, he agreed.

So, Paula approached me. She told me the story of the kittens and pleaded with me to take one. I was such a sucker for abandoned and at-risk pets, I said yes immediately without talking to my husband about it. Bob was an animal lover, but never had a cat as a pet. After I talked with him, he agreed that we could take her but only if she was an outdoor cat. I hated this, but agreed because it was better than having her drown in the river.

Oh, Boots. She was a black and white wonder. She had a black and white face, with soft white fur around her nose and mouth, and the longest white whiskers I had ever seen, even as a kitten. But it was her legs that were her true distinguishing feature. Her legs were black but turned white halfway down, as if someone had drawn a line in the middle of her leg to mark off the black from the white. While Socks probably would have been a more appropriate name, we named her Boots.

In the early days outside, she slept in the cottonwood trees on our property. When I came out to feed her, this tiny kitten would leap out of the tree she was sleeping in and race to me, loudly purring and snuggling around my ankles. Reluctantly wild and free, she sought all of the love she could get at feeding times. I, of course, sought her out at other times during the day to give her love and attention.

While Boots roamed the three-acre property freely, her favorite place to be, like mine, was in the garden. She would sniff the flowers with contentment, but it was the vegetable garden to which she was truly drawn. Beginning in early summer, she would walk the rows of vegetables, sniffing and admiring the green beans, corn, onions, green peppers, and zucchini. But it was the tomatoes that were her favorite. Large, beefsteak succulents bursting with ripeness, by midsummer, she just couldn't resist.

One early morning, I walked the vegetable garden as I usually did in the summer, admiring my wonderful produce. When I got to the tomato section, I stopped short. Every large, beautiful tomato now had a single bite taken out of each of them. I didn't have to think twice about what had done this. I knew. After weeks of watching her sniff the produce and purr around each of the plants, I had no doubt it was Boots. The reluctant wild in her just couldn't resist. So much for my tomato harvest that year. I saved as many of the tomatoes as I could, but my harvest that year was less than spectacular. But Boots? Boots was thoroughly fulfilled and happy.

As the Fall approached, I pleaded with my husband to let Boots be an indoor kitty. I couldn't bear for her to be outside in the cold Illinois winter weather. It took a while to wear him down, but reluctantly, he agreed. What a life she had!! A soft bed, toys, the run of the house, including permission to sleep on any piece of furniture she wanted, Boots was so appreciative, she wanted to earn her keep.

Since we lived in a farmhouse, in the late Fall, I would set mousetraps in the house in anticipation of the field mouse migration to warmth before the winter. My nutty Penny dog, who got into everything and was afraid of nothing, had no desire to approach the mouse traps. I'm pretty sure, knowing her, that she was smart enough to be afraid of them and what they could do to her. Boots, however, was on high alert. Too refined to be a mouser, she waited that Fall to see what would happen when the field mice migrated into our farmhouse.

On multiple mornings, as I was making breakfast, Boots would stroll into the kitchen, so proud, with a mousetrap in her mouth containing a mangled mouse. She, of course, never did the mouse work, but was so happy to present the kill! I know she thought to herself, "What a woman!" It occurred to me after a few days, not only was she presenting me with a present, she was, in her mind, presenting me with breakfast. If this was a suitable breakfast for a cat, certainly it would be a suitable breakfast for her favorite human!

Over the years together—there were 18 in all—Boots and Penny became fast friends. They played together and snuggled together. Often, in a moment of intimacy, Boots would knead Penny's hips with her paws, bringing Penny temporary relief from the arthritis that was besieging her. They both were completely happy to have each other. What an odd couple they were. Penny was wild and nutty. Boots was calm, aloof, and calculating.

Boots had no idea that in her later years, she would become the ever-famous Boots Penn, revered in the halls of Hubbard Trail Middle School. Her antics legendary because of my stories about her, she would become the topic of hallway conversation for years to come.

Penny remained, always, my smart, wild, loving, nutty dog.

Over the years, I became a cat collector. Yes, I was one of those crazy cat ladies. In my adult life, I have had seventeen cats, thirteen of whom lived together at one time. "Why? Why would you do that?" some of my friends would ask. My answer was that I wasn't so sure that I found them, as much as they found me. They were all strays in search of love and a home, with the exception of three pet store rescues I was sure were headed for animal experimentation labs.

Among the notables was Hairy. A golden, long-haired Tabby-Manx mix, Hairy's long tail jutted high in the air, and then as if snapped in half, pointed straight down. I don't know if it was his odd tail or his odd personality that made him a loner. When the other cats tried to befriend him, repeatedly he pounded them on the head with his paw. "You know," I used to tell him often, "nobody likes you. I mean, I do, but none of the other cats like you. Why can't you just be nice?"

Well, it turns out he was eventually nice, just not with another cat.

One Easter, I gave my youngest daughter a stuffed bunny as part of her Easter basket. Jamie loved that bunny, and so, apparently, did Hairy. In the weeks that followed, the bunny, which was in my daughter's room, would show up in odd places in the house—the sofa, the top of the recliner, the kitchen counter, and the table. I would, of course, pick it up and return it to Jamie's room. When I asked Jamie why her bunny was laying in every room of the house, she said she didn't know anything about it. She always kept her stuffed bunny on the shelf in her room.

Soon, the howling began. I would be awakened at night to the sound of an ear-piercing, guttural howl. Who could that be? Was one of the cats hurt? With thirteen of them, it was hard to tell who was in distress. So, I would get up in the night and do a safety check. Each night, though, they all seemed fine, sleeping soundly.

One night, as I came down the stairs to do my ever-frequent safety check, I stumbled upon an intimate scene I would rather not have seen. There was Hairy, howling, and having his way with Jamie's bunny on the top of the recliner! That was what that ever-frequent howling was about!! Since nobody was hurt, and it appeared that Hairy had finally connected with something, I went back to bed and had a pleasant night's sleep.

Over the years, Hairy frequently had his way with that bunny, not only during the night, but during the day. The bunny no longer was Jamie's, but Hairy's, and after the frequent bunny violations, Jamie was just fine with that! The poor stuffed bunny, a happy Easter gift, became known in our house, tongue-in-cheek, as Hairy's Bitch.

Once Hairy became enamored and intimate with his bunny, he seemed to be nicer to the other cats. The power of frequent sex with someone he truly cared about seemed to work wonders for Hairy, as I suppose it can for any of us. When Hairy was cremated, the object of his affection was cremated with him. It certainly seemed to be the right decision at the time, and I am sure, ultimately, Hairy was very pleased, too.

I adopted Scratchy when his owners were in the middle of a contentious divorce. Among the many things they fought about was the damage Scratchy inflicted on their house. Though they had him since he was a kitten, as the tension in their household escalated, so had the damage to their belongings. Clearly affected by their discontent, Scratchy expressed his anxiety by clawing their sofa, their chairs, their bed, and, the ultimate insult, completely destroying the pool table in the man cave. After that event, he was going to be euthanized.

Debbie did feel bad about that and reached out to my roommate, who worked for her, to see if she would adopt Scratchy. And yes, we both agreed to take him.

One of the lucky thirteen, Scratchy was an enormous, gold, very tall, long-haired Tabby. Besides his beautiful gold fur, his gentle eyes were also gold. When he came to our house, he immediately bonded with the other cats. A gentle soul, he was, it seemed, a spiritual leader. He was calming and brought peace to all of the cats, and to me as well.

It should come as no surprise, given his temperament, that Scratchy was my Christmas kitty. How he loved Christmas!! When the boxes of decorations were brought into the house, he would jump into each box, sniffing the contents. While I was decorating, he would lay in the boxes and purr in anticipation of the magical Christmas season about to happen! After the Christmas tree was put up—a live tree, of course-the lights strung, and the ornaments put up, Scratchy would lay beside the tree, gazing wistfully at the lights. Of all the seasons of the year, this clearly was his favorite. When we watched A Christmas Story, as we did every year, Scratchy would lay on the floor beside us, actually watching the movie! He was as enamored of Ralphie and his family as we were!

I dreaded when the Christmas season was over, and I needed to take down the tree and box up the decorations. Yes, it was sad for me, but it was devastating for Scratchy. Poor buddy, he was inconsolable. The decorations removed and boxed, Scratchy would cry and jump into the boxes to keep me from packing them. Oh, and the tree! When I had to climb the ladder to take the lights and ornaments down, he would climb the ladder after me, clawing at my legs! Keep in mind, since I had adopted him, feeling the calm and peace in my house, he never once scratched a single thing. But he did scratch at me when Christmas was over and the magic was coming to an end. His sadness at the end of the season was equal to his joy at the beginning of it.

I still keep the Christmas hat Scratchy wore willingly every year for his Christmas photo. He was so happy!! I, too, am happy when I look at his hat and remember the complete joy he brought to Christmas.

After my roommate's dog, Buc, died, I was lost. A Chesapeake Bay Retriever who lived to be seventeen years old, he was my best buddy. I took him on daily walks and adventures, and though he wasn't my dog, he felt like mine. After a couple of months, I knew I would have to have another dog in my life. So, I looked aggressively for a new dog companion. Always a shelter pet rescuer, I broke with tradition just this once and found a local Chocolate Lab breeder.

Stephanie, the breeder, was a love, and it was clear that she loved her puppies. Fifteen in all in the litter, it was obvious she loved each and every one of them. Among the other things she did was let the puppies swim in her backyard in-ground swimming pool. They were so cute, paddling around in that pool, all 15 of them!

Choosing among them was hard. I knew I wanted a

small one, and then seeing them all, I knew I wanted a second puppy, this one a larger one. Really? Two dogs? What was I thinking? As it turns out, my thinking was right. My youngest daughter, Jamie, was with me when we picked out the puppies. Jamie, too, was sad when Buc died. Buc was Jamie's childhood companion. They were truly bonded, and she missed him. While there could be no replacement for Buc, she, too, was ready for another dog in her life.

We met the parent dogs that day. The father was a beautiful AKC registered field champion Lab and his mate was also a beautiful AKC registered Chocolate Lab. Both of them, while powerful in stature, were on the smaller side of 75 lbs. So, I surmised that the puppies I chose would be about that size and weight as full-grown adults.

How did I choose from among them? Billy, the smaller of the two, while slightly neurotic, was outgoing and willing to please. Jack was doe-eyed, reserved, and the largest pup in the litter. Ahh, I knew these two were to become my new puppies.

On the drive home, my roommate was driving while Jamie and I held the puppies in the back seat. While Jack was to become Jamie's dog, I held him on the trip home, trying to comfort him as he whimpered continually on the three-mile trip back to our home. I will never be sure exactly what made him cry. A sensitive dog, as I later learned, maybe he missed his home with his brothers and sisters. Maybe he suddenly missed his owner, Stephanie. Or maybe he was just unsure about what his future would now be like with me. Billy, sitting comfortably in Jamie's lap and looking out the window, was ever the intellectual, evaluating his new experience with all the analysis of a professional accountant.

Oh, what a joy these puppies were! Pudgy, roly-poly pups, they explored their new environment with enthusiasm. Innocent and unabashed, they sniffed everything and greeted my thirteen cats with casual caution. Not exactly sure what they were, the cats nosed them and then moved on. The cats, normally defensive when a new animal was introduced into the household, were thrown off guard by the puppies' casualness. They circled Jack and Billy, decided they were harmless, and then resumed what they had been doing before the puppies entered the house.

That evening, I set up the puppies' den in the kitchen, which had a door blocking them from the rest of the house. We still had to work on the house-breaking thing. I still was uncertain how the cats might react to them in the night, though I suppose if they really wanted to get into the kitchen, the cats could have jumped through the open half-wall that separated the kitchen from the living room. But they didn't. They thought the puppies were interesting and different, but posed no threat, so ultimately, they just didn't care.

I had the pups AKC registered. Their official names were Jamie's Jack Dawson, named after the lead character in James Cameron's movie Titanic, and Porter's Prince William, named after my brother who was The Prince, the favored one in our childhood home.

Although they had a huge yard to play in and gardens to explore, I took the puppies for daily walks in the neighborhood. Dark chocolate with blue eyes that eventually turned to a dead grass color, I suppose the walks were not as much about their exercise, as my pride in how cute they were. The walks took a long time because everyone we encountered had to pet them, love them up, and tell me how adorable they were.

As they grew, and they DID grow to be much larger than I ever imagined, they began to exhibit typical Lab behavior. They were chewers. Enormous at three months, both of them, they wreaked havoc on my house and my furniture. I shouldn't say "they". It was Jack. You have to remember their unique personalities. Billy was the observer, the analytical accountant, and the voice of reason. He was just neurotic enough to worry about all of the bad things Jack would do and what the consequences would be. He, of course, felt the obligation to report every infraction to me when I came home from work. Circling my round kitchen table repeatedly, he would talk to me in a voice reminiscent of Dustin Hoffman's autistic savant character, Raymond, in the movie Rainman. "I'm a little bit nervous today. A little bit nervous. Yeah, it was Jack. Yeah, it was Jack. Shouldn't have done it. Shouldn't have done it. I told him. I told him. We're going to be in trouble today. Going to be in trouble today. Shouldn't have done it, Jack."

Jack was my doe-eyed, free spirit. While reserved and sweet, he went with the flow, always. If the spirit moved him, he went with it. Over the first six months, these are the things he destroyed with his obsessive need to chew. My newly-laid tile in the kitchen, my kitchen table (he ate huge bites out of the edge of the table and the rungs of the chairs), my wooden porch swing, the corners of my outdoor deck, the wooden breadbox I had on my counter (and the contents), my reading glasses, a sprinkler head, venetian blinds, the patio door screen, my outside lilac bush, my dandelion picker, my binoculars, and the list goes on and on. While other dogs have chew bones, both Jack and Billy (Billy undoubtedly talked into it by Jack) would select pieces of chopped, oak firewood to chew on. Perhaps it was that special oak taste that attracted them. More often than not I would come home from work to find oak logs and splintered wood covering my kitchen floor.

On several—no—on many occasions, after one of Jack's destructive or wild episodes, I would talk to him as he stared at me with dopey-eyed innocence. "Why do you do these things, Jack? WHY do you do these things? This is what a Bad Dog looks like, Jack. He looks just like you!" Though he didn't answer me, I knew what his answer would be. "I just felt the strong need to do it."

Poor Billy! Ever the voice of conscience, he sweated through each event, neurotically circling the table as he gave his report. Billy was never the perpetrator, but always the reporter.

And who was my favorite of the two? Jack. I loved them both, but Jack was clearly my favorite, although the clearly logical, conscience-ridden Billy should have stolen my heart and taken the top slot. Jack was a dopey-eyed, free, untamed spirit. I admired him for that. Maybe I secretly wished I could be just a little like him. When I would pet Jack and tell him I loved him, I would then pet Billy and tell him, I love you, too, Billy." Over the years, the saying was always "And you, too, Billy."

Unlike the 75-pound expectation based on their parents' size and weight, Billy and Jack grew and grew and grew. Tall enough to impressively clean off any counter or table, they weighed in at 120 and 110 pounds. Tall and lean, they were ponies. Ponies living in my house!

Jack grew so fast, he developed shoulder issues. At less than a year old, I took him to Colorado State University for evaluation. Surgery was the solution. After his surgery, I was worried about him coming out on a gurney and carrying him to the car. To my surprise, when they released him, he came bounding around the corner, racing full speed. The other dog owners in the waiting room, waiting for their dogs' evaluations, quickly picked up their dogs and held them to protect them from this huge, wild dog running through the room. While he was no threat to the other dogs, he was, I have to admit, an imposing figure.

I was supposed to keep Jack in a "cone of shame" to keep him from licking his incisions. This did not work for him! He wildly bashed his cone into my kitchen cabinets, his cone clearly too restrictive for his free spirit. What to do? Since the objective was to keep him from scratching and licking his stitches, I had an idea. Hmm. I bought a man's T-shirt and cut off the bottom to make a midriff. No opportunity for licking or scratching the stitches, he could clearly retain his freedom and his ever-important macho status! He was ultimately happy and healed quickly.

Shortly after Jack was healed from his surgery, we had another major incident. Ever the cruiser, he meandered into a room where I had a cat box. There were five cat boxes in all in the house, but Jack chose the one in my office. Sticking his head in the box to savor the nut rolls, his huge head became stuck in the litterbox top. Flailing and anxious, he ran downstairs to the kitchen, his den, and began banging the litterbox top against the cabinets. Try as I might, I couldn't release the litterbox top from his huge head. Fearful he would completely obliterate my kitchen cabinets, while Billy ran in anxious circles around the new kitchen table I purchased after Jack ate pieces of my old one, I called my oldest daughter, Lisa, to help me out. Living in an apartment down the street from me and working from home that day, she quickly came to the house. After petting him to calm him down and forcefully pulling on the litterbox top, she freed him! So happy for his freedom, he ran outside to the yard and gardens that gave him peace, lying beside his favorite rose tree. As for me, I got to clean up the litter box contents that were strewn from the office all the way down to the kitchen.

Once again, I told him, semi-sternly, "This is what a Bad Dog looks like, Jack. He looks just like you!"

As if Jack wasn't dopey-eyed already, he developed a condition known as entropion. His bottom eyelids rolled in, the eyelashes rubbing his eyes and causing so much irritation, he looked like he was constantly crying. So off we went to the vet—again. Corrective surgery pulled Jack's eyelids down, resulting in a slight V-shape along the lower lid. Dopey-eyed before, Jack was a very dopey-eyed Jack now. At times, his eyes looked more like a Bloodhound's than a Labs. If he was irresistible before the surgery, he was even more so with his new, magnified, dopey-eyed look.

Earlier, I said that Billy was never the perpetrator of the disastrous deeds in our household, but rather the ritualistic reporter. What I should have said was that he wasn't the conscious perpetrator.

One Sunday afternoon after I had baked cookies, I ran a load of dishes in the dishwasher. After the cycle was completed, I opened the dishwasher door, pulled out the bottom rack, and began putting the clean dishes away.

That afternoon Billy was wearing a choke-chain collar. I never did like those much, although I guess they are appropriate for some dogs on some occasions. My taste ran to the soft, multi-colored collars that showed off my boys' deep chocolate color. The choke chain Billy was wearing had belonged to Buc. Billy was wearing it only because, like a good mom, I was washing his other collars, of which there were many. It seemed like every time I went to the pet store, I was buying new collars for Billy and Jack. I just couldn't get enough of buying new "clothes" for my boys.

As I reached down to remove a couple of dinner plates, I accidently banged them together loudly. Startled by the noise, Billy, who was napping on the floor near the dishwasher, jumped up quickly to get away from the noise. As he jumped up, the ring on his choke-chain collar got stuck on the dishwasher rack. At 110 lbs., even though he was the smaller of the two dogs, Billy was tall and powerful. Feeling the resistance against the choke chain, he pulled with a mighty force to free himself. I, of course, focusing on putting the plates away, didn't see that his collar was caught on the rack. Despite the extreme force, he didn't free his collar from the rack, but, instead, pulled the entire rack, loaded with dishes, completely out of the dishwasher. Now in full-blown panic, Billy did what he always did. He neurotically began circling my round kitchen table, dragging the dishwasher rack with him. Each time he circled, he ran faster, the loaded rack swaying from side to side. By the time I realized he was hooked on the rack and managed to free him, every single plate and every glass in that bottom rack was smashed, glass flying everywhere.

In his best Rainman voice, a very worried Billy, afraid he was in trouble, said, "Not my fault today. Not my fault. Didn't mean to. Didn't mean to. Didn't mean to!" I do believe it was after that event that Billy began to get grey hairs on his muzzle.

To say that Billy and Jack were spoiled would be an understatement. And why wouldn't I spoil them? Their innocent, unending affection for me was as enormous as they were, and I gladly reciprocated.

One Saturday, when they were full-grown dogs, I decided that dogs that enormous shouldn't have to be cooped up all day in a kitchen den. What they needed was a dog door so that they could come and go freely during the day while I was at work. Great idea! Why didn't I think of that before? Motivated, I made a trip to PetSmart, and knowing how big my dogs were, I bought the largest dog door they had. Excited for them, I immediately installed it when I came home. Designed to fit a sliding glass patio door, I was sure this would do the trick.

Now it was time to show the dogs how to use it. To demonstrate, I crawled through the opening myself from the kitchen onto the deck, hoping they were observing. Once outside, I called to them. Billy, ever cautious and analytical, stood staring at it as if sizing up its dimensions. Jack, my free-spirited Jack, on the other hand, came bounding from the kitchen through the dog door to greet me.

Only one problem. Jack was so enormous and his shoulders so broad, he got stuck halfway through the dog door. Even the largest patio door was too small to fit his massive body. Now firmly wedged, it took me a full five minutes to release him from its unwanted embrace. Disappointed, I returned the dog door to PetSmart that afternoon.

Not one to be daunted by adversity, I just knew there had to be a solution. Putting on my creative carpenter's cap, I had an idea. I went to the Home Depot and bought a hollow door. After measuring Jack's height and the breadth of his shoulders, I cut an opening large enough for him to get through. Complete with a waterproof flap and a carpet piece that hung on the kitchen side of the door, the door was hinged to swing out when I wanted to go outside from the kitchen onto the deck and into the yard. Problem solved! The dogs were ecstatic.

That summer I also built them a log cabin dog house, complete with inside baseboards, a chimney, and a deck beside the house where they could lounge on beach mats under a large umbrella. The only time they ever went in that dog house was when I was working in the yard, and even then, they were more content to be following me through the yard and gardens. Still, I was pleased with my carpentry gifts to them.

Bath time for the dogs was truly an experience. When Jack and Billy were puppies, once a week I could put them both in the shower with me to bathe them. As Labs, of course, they loved the water. As they grew to be adult dogs resembling ponies, there was barely room for one of them and me. Billy, of course, would sit calmly while I bathed him. Always thinking, I was sure his mind was occupied with the rules for the most efficient way to bathe a dog, calculated down to each soaping and each rinse.

Dopey-eyed Jack, though wild and spirited most of the time, savored his bath time. Leaning against the ceramic tile, his eyes half-closed, he would inhale deeply the aroma of the peppermint shampoo and conditioner I lavished on him. His afterbath ritual was completed with a rub of coconut cream to soften his large, rough paws. So relaxed from his bath experience, Jack could hardly walk up the stairs to his den. A good nap following his pseudo-spa experience was always in order for him.

As for me, it took longer to clean up the bathroom after the bath than to bathe them. Enormous amounts of hair were stuck to the shower floor and on the walls where they shook violently after getting out of the shower. Emerging from this frequent bath event, each time, I looked like a survivor from the sinking of the Titanic.

Ever the writer, I used to make up stories about Billy and Jack. Their personalities each so dynamic and unique, in my mind, I just had to sketch them.

Here is how I pictured them. My wild and free Jack was a graduate of Automotive and Diesel College. A certified mechanic, he worked a second job as a bouncer in a Longmont strip club called Bella's. Though actually sweet in nature, his large, imposing, muscular physique made him perfect for the job. The extra money he earned went to fixing up his outdoor log cabin man-cave he shared with Billy. Complete with cable TV and a sound system, their weekend kegger parties were famous in the neighborhood.

On the weekends, Jack drove my Ford Ranger truck. Cruising Main Street, which was the "in" place to be on the weekends, he wore a white T-Shirt (to accentuate his chocolate color) with his smokes tucked in the rolled-up sleeve. What a catch he thought he was with his sunglasses, his truck, and his impressive dark chocolate!

Billy was a graduate of what he referred to as Sniff Dog College. A search and rescue dog, he took great pride in the discipline it took to approach dangerous locations and save lives. His greatest pride was in his orange vest that displayed his professional status. For years, Billy was enamored with the Little Red Headed Girl, an Irish Setter who lived down the block. He always wanted to wear his orange vest, hoping she would be impressed with his education, professional training, and ultimately, his sweet disposition.

Surprisingly, Billy was clearly my athlete. Obsessed with his balls (!!), he could retrieve like no other. Focused and disciplined, he would back up from me and wait until I threw a straight-line pitch which he caught solidly in his mouth. He never missed. With such pride in his skill, he would run back to me and drop the ball at my feet. Obsessively, he would do this over and over until he was completely exhausted.

My Jack was a football guy. When I poised his orange football for a throw, he would prance his feet like a two-point stance linebacker waiting for action. When I would forcefully throw the ball, he would catch it, prance around the yard as if in the end zone, and then drop it. His work now done after having caught the ball once, he would retreat to the garden to sit under his rose tree. Jack was too free-spirited to ever be a real retriever.

As the dogs got older, they each began to exhibit physical issues. Jack's were the most pronounced. So large and so wild, his cruciate ligaments became compromised. Too old for surgery, we chose palliative care. I bought him a red vest with a handle I could use to hold him up. Poor Buddy, every time he had to go to the bathroom, I had to go with him to "suitcase" him, as we called it, to stabilize his back legs.

When he was 11, Jack seemed really tired all the time and had a chronic cough. I took him to our local vet. Upon examination, she told me to take him to Colorado State University for evaluation. After radiographs and ultrasounds, I learned that Jack had cardiomyopathy. Most likely a genetic pre-disposition, I was devastated by the diagnosis. Jack, my dopey-eyed Jack, was in jeopardy. His heart-related medicines cost over $300 a month, but I didn't care. I wanted my Jack with me for as long as I could have him.

Often, in the days after his diagnosis, Jack would walk to my garden and lay beside his favorite rose tree. He loved that tree, and I loved that it brought him peace. Sometimes, I would stare at him lying by that tree, and would wonder what he was thinking.

Jack was with me for almost a year after his diagnosis. Tired and not so wild, he loved to lay on the deck, with the fire in my firepit warming him. Often when we were out there together, I would play Alan Jackson's album Precious Memories. Though tired and struggling, he loved to hear the hymns. He would open his eyes, sigh, and embrace the music that soothed him.

One night, I sat beside him and put my arms around him. I asked him to give me a sign for what he wanted me to do. I desperately wanted him to tell me when he thought it was time.

As it turns out, my youngest daughter, Jamie, was staying with me for a while before she moved to Seattle. Jack, of course, was always Jamie's dog. She loved him and doted on him as I did. On one of those days, Jack was lying on the floor, too weak to get up. Together, we lifted him up and carried him to the car to take him to the vet. After examining him, our sweet vet said that his organs were shutting down. His heart was no longer able to sustain him. Euthanasia was his humane destiny. Oh God, selfishly, I wasn't ready to let my Jack go. I told her I just wanted one more night with him, and I would bring him in the morning. Jamie and I carried him back to the car and drove him home.

Peaceful in his kitchen den, I sat with Jack, petted him, and reminded him of all the crazy, destructive things he had done in his life. More importantly, I also told him how much love and joy he had brought to my life. He had, in fact, changed me over the course of his life. He made me a freer spirit, just like him, and I loved him for that.

At 2:00 AM, I woke with a start. I needed to check on Jack! When I went to the kitchen den, Billy, for once, was sitting calmly on his bed, looking at Jack. When I touched Jack, I knew he was gone. Sobbing on his body, I knew what he had done for me. Jack knew that euthanizing him would kill me, but I would do it to give him the final peace he so needed. My boy. My Jack. Sensitive and soft-hearted, I knew that he wanted to keep me safe from pain, just as he always had. In the morning, Jamie and I carried Jack's body to the car and drove him to the vet. Our vet said that in all her years of practice, this was the only time in her career a pet died the night before it was scheduled to be euthanized. I smiled. That was my big-hearted Jack, always thinking of me.

Of course, after Jack's death, I was overcome with sadness. I walked the gardens, looking at all the plants he loved so much. I missed him. Walking by his favorite rose tree, I spoke to him. "Ok, buddy. I know you are in a different place now, but could you send me a sign that you are ok? I really, really need this. I miss you."

Two days later, while I was sitting on my deck, looking at the flowers in my garden, a dragonfly flew close to my face, as if trying to get my attention. It was beautiful, but somewhat annoying. Soon this dragonfly and another were flying again close to my face. What was this? It suddenly dawned on me. It was Jack! This was the sign I so desperately wanted from him! I pondered this wonderful realization and was now at peace. The dragonfly is the symbol of change and transformation, and I don't think he could have chosen a better sign to tell me that he was ok.

Billy was lonely without Jack. He no longer wanted to play ball or sniff the yard and gardens. Depressed, he now spent most of his time lying on his bed in the kitchen den he and Jack had shared for so many years. His spiritual savior came, of all places, from my cat Pickle.

Pickle was my last and final rescue cat. When I rescued him, I already had twelve cats. The last thing I needed was another one. Knowing I was a cat lover, a friend from work approached me and told me the story of Pickle. Originally named Pixel because of his black color, Pickle grew up in a house in the mountains. An indoor and outdoor cat, Pickle's adventures were shared with his constant companion, a gold tabby named Dora. At the age of 7, on one of their outdoor adventures, Dora was eaten by a mountain lion. Fearful that Pickle would suffer the same fate, and because she had acquired two large dogs, Pickle's owner had been searching for a new home for him without success. She was afraid she was going to have to take him to the humane society.

Reluctantly, I told my co-worker that I would take Pickle if, and only if, she couldn't find a home for him.

Pickle and I instantly bonded. We felt like long-time soulmates. A list maker like me, Pickle had a strict agenda for what needed to be done each day. If I wasn't working in my office by 9:00 AM, he would stand next to me, mentally tapping his foot impatiently. Frequently, I would stack papers by my desk that needed to be filed. When the stack reached a certain height, Pickle would come in the office and begin to scatter the stack with his paws, as if to say, "Enough, already!! File this stuff!" He was, in every sense of the word, my office manager.

But Pickle was also sensitive to my moods. He seemed to sense when I needed comforting and would jump, purring, into my lap. At night, he always slept comfortably curled around my head. A garden lover like me, he would take walks with me in the flowers and vegetables, paying careful attention as I explained what each flower and vegetable was. Heeling like a dog, he stayed right beside me on these ever-frequent walks.

So, it came as no surprise to me that Pickle was the one who sensed Billy's sadness and sought to comfort him. He would lay next to Billy on his bed, offering Billy the companionship he was so missing. Over the next few weeks, Billy began to perk up. He resumed his ball playing and could be seen walking the gardens with Pickle at his side.

Perhaps the most touching moments were when Billy and Pickle curled up together under Jack's favorite rose tree. I think they each sensed Jack's spirit there and were completely content to share that experience together.

It may sound strange, but over the years my pets have taught me to be a better person. I have learned many, many lessons from them. Pets don't care what you look like, how much money you have, or what you do for a living. Their lives are simpler and, ultimately, deeper than that. They enjoy every bite of their food and embrace each day with complete joy. Even if you are away from them for an hour, they act as if you have been gone for a year and greet you with unreserved love and unbridled enthusiasm. They don't measure their actions by what someone will think of them. They just act, as the spirit moves them, and take complete joy in their actions. Pets love you without judgement, and love you honestly, completely, and consistently, regardless of whatever may be going on in your life. Pets, ultimately, compel you to see the world through their simple, innocent eyes.

From my vantage point, that's a pretty darn good view.

Ms. Ivy Pole

In the past, intimacy has been something that *I* have chosen to have with someone. I have always chosen where and how and for how long. There are a select few with whom I have shared shower time and bathroom intimacy; always, of course, my choice. I have never, however, had someone stand beside me while I slept, nor have I been forced to include them in every waking (and sleeping) activity that I engaged in. Never. Until this week.

After emergency colon surgery, I woke up to find myself intimately tethered to a complete stranger. Six foot-six, unattractively tall and skinny, her face was not on what would have been her head, but on her belly. Ms. Ivy Pole, as I came to call her over time, seemed pleasant enough, even if she wasn't much to look at. Standing sentry while I drifted in and out of consciousness, she willingly held my two intravenous bags and catheter bag while I slept. She was ok, I guess, if you have to be stuck with someone not of your own choosing.

While silent most of the time, her opinions were obvious, however. As I struggled to sit up, post-surgery, to eat my first meal, her red numeric eyes blinked and her digital mouth smirked as if to say, "Really? Is that the best they could do for you for food? Cream of wheat and apple juice? I can give you better nutrition in these bags of mine than what you are getting with that stuff!" Well, I thought, it's not your choice, so you should keep your opinions to yourself. I stared at her, but, since it was early in our relationship, I said nothing and returned to my meal—such as it was.

In the mid-afternoon on that first hospital day, I lay on the bed listening to the TV and dozing on and off. I hurt and was sleepy. When I was finally in a deep sleep, the sound of screaming filled the room and woke me with a start. What? What was that? I turned to my left and saw that it was Ivy! Clearly upset, her red eyes flashed, and she kept screaming without pause. Not knowing quite what to do, I rang for the nurse.

After a few minutes, the nurse came in the room and pressed the side of Ivy's mouth to silence her. "One of your IV bags is empty, so that noise tells us we need to change it out. When that happens, just do what you just did and call us. But, if you want that noise to stop, just push this button right here, but don't forget to call us."

When the nurse left, I looked at Ivy, said nothing, but thought, "Isn't there a better way to do this? I'm sure you care about my meds and my nutrition, but do you have to scream??"

My first road trip with Ivy came less than 12 hours after my surgery. Accompanied by two occupational therapists who needed to assess my mobility capabilities, the four of us proceeded down the hallway toward the stairwell. Since I would, upon discharge from the hospital, be recuperating at my daughter's house, I had to demonstrate my ability to navigate stairs.

I quickly got the impression that Ivy didn't like this foursome at all. Only wanting it to be the two of us, she dragged her feet, tugged at my tubes, and refused, without strong persuasion, to cross the threshold to the stairwell. As I climbed the stairs to demonstrate my ability to do so, Ivy was restrained by one of the occupational therapists. Although she didn't say anything, I could tell by the flashing digits on her face that she was very, very upset. Clearly sulking, she was co-operative but extremely quiet on the trip back to the room.

It was after this walk that our relationship began to get a little strange, by normal standards. I am not one who likes to be confined or alone. With the exception of my daughter and a couple of friends who came to visit me, I was on my own, except for the nurses who came in to check my vitals periodically. I missed my dogs, missed my home, and had no use for either the needles in my arms or the ten staples on my abdomen. To make matters worse, I was tethered to a petulant child that I never asked to be with. But—and this is the sad part—she was my only constant company.

Feeling a bit like Tom Hanks talking to Wilson the volleyball in the movie Cast Away, I felt compelled to talk OUT LOUD to Ivy. "Did you really have to act that way with the occupational therapists? They were just doing their jobs, and you didn't make it easy on them. While we're on the subject, you haven't made it exactly easy on me, either. I know you only have enough juice in you to last two hours, but when I plug you in, do you have to pull the tubes in my arms? You wound the tubes around my feet when I got up to get my lunch tray, and then you kept making remarks about what I was eating. I didn't ask for this stuff, but it's what I get and the less you comment on it, the better off we both will be." There—I said what was on my mind and clearly felt better.

Several hours later, it was time for a shower. I DREADED this, not because I didn't want or need a shower, but because

I knew what it meant. Ivy had to go with me. Carefully, I unplugged her from the wall and pushed her gently into the bathroom, closing the door behind us. "Alright, "I said, "listen up. I'm not sure you want to be in here with me any more than I want you be in here. But I don't want some mechanical voyeur checking me out when I take my clothes off, so I am turning your face toward the wall, and don't think of arguing with me. I know that sounds a little harsh, but that's the way it is going to be."

Seconds after I turned her face to the wall and began to take off my gown, Ivy began to scream. "What now?" I said, "My med bags are full, so I know that's not it. What is wrong with you?!" Fortunately, my gown was still more on than off, and so I turned her slightly from the wall so that I could see her face. Aha—despite having been plugged in for a while, her juice was low, and she was terribly displeased. "Too bad, Ivy. You are not going to scream when I shower." I reached over and touched the side of her mouth to silence her.

The shower was problematic. Though she was quiet, Ivy pulled at my tubes and my catheter and generally made my shower a disaster. But—I was clean. After I put on a fresh gown, I pushed Ivy from the bathroom, plugged her into the wall, and looked her in the eyes. "Ok, doll," I said, "we're going to have to get some things worked out. Maybe you don't want to be with me anymore than I want to be with you, although you do seem to be quite possessive of me. Since you are nice enough to hold up all of my fluid bags, I'll do my best to make sure you have enough juice to sustain you. And, since you are staying up all night watching over me, I won't get upset if you scream when one of my fluid bags is empty. I'll just silence you for a while and call the nurse. Ok, about your comments on the food. I just got upset because I know you are right. The food is awful, and I don't want it either, but could you just keep your snide remarks to yourself?? Ok, how about this? How about if you and I take a walk together tomorrow, just the two of us?" After a few minutes, this conciliatory talk seemed to placate her. She was, it seemed, less stubborn and was quiet the rest of the night. She didn't even comment on my evening meal!

The next morning, as promised, Ivy and I took a long walk through the halls, just the two of us. She didn't drag her feet and didn't pull my tubes. We were making progress toward a sustainable relationship!!

Shortly after our walk, the nurse came in to remove my catheter. Yes! One less tube to trip over! But I knew what this meant. With IV fluids being pumped in to me with a vengeance, I would be making many trips to the bathroom with Ivy in tow. Time for another talk.

"Ok, so here's the good news. You don't have to hold up my catheter bag anymore. Isn't that great? Geez, it must have been kind of gross for you. Of course, at least it wasn't blood, right? But here's the bad news. Without the catheter, we're going to make a lot of trips to the bathroom, including during the night. I will wake you when I have to go, although you don't seem to sleep much, do you? But here's the thing. Just like with the shower stuff, I don't want you looking at me when I go, so you're going to face the wall, ok? It's nothing personal—I just don't want it to be personal, if you know what I mean. Good. I'm glad we had this talk."

Except for dragging her feet across the threshold, Ivy did pretty well on her bathroom visits. She faced the wall while I chatted on and on about the nurses and some of the patients in the rooms we walked by every day. "Did you hear that young girl yelling 'help me' in room 410? Wonder what her deal is? I heard the nurse say she was going to give her a shot of Haldol. You know, they give that to people who are having psychotic episodes."

Suddenly, there was a knock on the bathroom door. "Porter, are you in there?"

"Ah, yeah, "I said.

"It's Shyla. Just remember we have to measure your output, so be sure to go in that urine tray."

Annoyed, I told Ivy I'd like to measure Shyla's output! What a pain to be so micromanaged!! Wonder if she heard me talking to you?

"What?" Shyla said.

"Oh," I said," I'll be right out."

"Ivy, I guess we'll have to talk more quietly. I don't want them to give me Haldol shot because they think I'm having a psychotic episode for talking to you. I'm not nuts, you know. Just lonely. I'll bet you get lonely sometimes, too."

On the third hospital night, I woke up at about 11:30. "Ivy," I said, "are you awake? I thought so. Guess what the nurse told me tonight? They're going to take out my IV's tomorrow. Great news, right? You won't have any more work to do! No more bathroom visits, no more walks, no more shower time. Sounds good, don't you think?"

The silence was deafening. I knew she was thinking about what that meant.

As promised, the next day Michelle, my nurse, came in and removed my intravenous catheters. She removed the tubes from Ivy and pushed her in the corner, facing the wall. I was so excited! Freedom! I was one step closer to going home!

Energized, I took a long, unencumbered walk down the hospital corridors, passing the rooms Ivy and I had passed on our previous walks. But this walk was faster and more free!! When I returned to the room, I got to eat real food— no more soft diet. I texted my daughter to tell her that I was pretty sure I was going to be discharged the next day. Tired from my long corridor walk, I decided to take a nap.

If I had thought about it, I would have known what would happen next. I was awakened to the sound of screaming. I had been so happy with my new-found freedom that I forgot Ivy had been pushed in a corner, de-commissioned, and left without juice. Clearly, she was crushed to be cast aside like that without a single thought from me. I crossed the room, put my hand on her neck, gently pushed her beside my bed, and plugged her in. "That was insensitive of me. You may not have any work to do, but we can still be friends. I'm sorry."

Ivy stood sentry beside me that night. There was no work for her to do but watch over me as I slept, which, I must say, gave me great comfort.

Shortly before my discharge the next day, Ivy and I had a final talk. "You know, I didn't like you at first. I didn't choose you, but then, I guess you didn't choose me either. Truth is, you took good care of me (except for the screaming), and you were good company. I enjoyed our walks and talks together. I thought you were kind of funny looking at first and thought about what you would look like with a make-over. But you know what? You have a big heart and that is what matters most."

I think about Ivy from time to time. Hers is a life of service. She doesn't get to choose who she serves, but she serves them all well and equally. But—she's pretty darn opinionated and possessive, and before I left, I told her she really needs to work on that.

The Gift

I am, it turns out, a caregiver for my longtime friend and roommate who was diagnosed with Alzheimer's disease nine months ago. Over the years, I have been a musician, a teacher, an entrepreneur, a counselor, a corporate executive, and a writer. As I looked with excitement at my possibilities for the future, an Alzheimer's caregiver was not something I expected to be. As one of my friends, who is a caregiver for her father, said, "This is not a ticket I chose to buy, either, but I have it now and have to take the ride, nevertheless." How right she was.

Anyone who is a caregiver for someone with Alzheimer's disease knows about the emotional highs and low, lows that come with being a caregiver. The unwanted guest in my home challenges me in ways I never could have imagined. The face I see every day is a familiar one, but the behavior I see is clearly that of a stranger. Why has my friend of so many years been replaced by a five-year-old with no impulse control? Where did Nancy go and who is this child? I resent her, just want Nancy back, and want things to be as they always have been.

This morning, the enormity of the responsibility for looking after her and securing a future for her when I am unable to care for her ran over me like a fast-moving freight train. I was emotionally flattened. So, I cried. It was a shoulder-shaking cry, with tears of loss and tears of loneliness. I cried for the inevitable change in my life, as well as the change in hers. I cried for the memories we will no longer make together. She is gone, and a stranger I scarcely like has taken her place.

I had to take my dog to the vet for her shots and bloodwork. While I was waiting, I decided I would call an Alzheimer's counselor when I got back home. Feeling emotionally depleted, I needed someone to fill me back up. I needed kind words and support.

When I arrived back home, Nancy, my now five-year-old, was begging me to take her out for breakfast. Last night, she begged me to get her ice cream and candy and stuck her tongue out at me when I said I wouldn't. Clearly, I needed help from a professional to guide me through this emotional minefield. I needed to make the right decisions for her, and apparently, I didn't know how. Nancy said I was mean to her, and maybe she was right, but I don't want to be mean.

Needing some peace for myself, I suggested a compromise. "How about if we skip breakfast. I will take you to the grocery store, and you can pick out something you want." With a huge, childlike grin on her face, she said, "Yeah! Let's do that!" So much for calling the Alzheimer's counselor.

Wandering through the grocery store with a five-year-old devoid of impulse control is quite an adventure. Equally adventurous is my journey through the range of emotions I have as I guide this stranger safely through the grocery store isles.

Standing in line to check out, I glanced down at the contents of the buggy. Fried chicken, potato chips and dip, a red velvet cake, and a candy bar. What on earth was I doing to this woman-child? I was angry and frustrated. The world today was a very, very dark place indeed.

As I looked up, my eyes focused on the woman in front of me who was trying to check out. Dressed in jeans and a padded vest, she had such an extreme curvature in her spine that she was nearly bent in half. Extremely thin, except for the hump that consumed her back, I would guess she was somewhere in her mid to late eighties. She had dropped her grocery card and was trying to figure out how to pick it up. I bent down, picked it up, and handed it to her. Her sweet smile lit up her face, and she said, "Thank you, honey."

Her check out process took a while. Though she didn't have that many things, she was slow and unsteady. I didn't mind. I was in no hurry to go home and watch Nancy devour an entire cake. Finally, the clerk said, "That will be $32.62." Fumbling through her wallet, the woman pulled out a ten-dollar bill. "Oh," she said, "I left in such a hurry, I forgot the rest of my money." The clerk said," Do you want to leave your groceries with me and go back home to get the rest of your money? I'll keep them here for you until you get back."

"No," the woman said, "I can't do that. Maybe we can take some things out, but I really did need all of it."

Quickly, it occurred to me that there was no money to get. Ten dollars was all she had. I leaned over to the clerk and said, "I'll cover her groceries. She doesn't need to put anything back."

The woman looked at me and said, "You don't need to do that." "No," I said, "I don't need to do it. I want to do it," and gently touched her on the shoulder.

With a look of relief, she smiled at me, and said, "What can I do for you?" "What you can do," I said, "is have a wonderful day." Though it was Nov 14th, she hugged me hard and said, "Merry Christmas."

This frail woman had no idea what she had just done for me. The emotional fill-up I thought I would get from an Alzheimer's counselor came from her. I had been so angry and focused on my own seemingly miserable circumstances that I had forgotten to look closely at someone else and to give back just a little.

Gifts come to us sometimes in ways we never expect. This frail woman, whose name I will never know, was truly a gift I never expected to receive.

Suddenly, because of her, my world was no longer a dark place.

An Offer He Couldn't Refuse

My husband was a TV sports junkie. While a hard worker who engaged in many activities outside of work and a kind and attentive father, when sports events were on TV – ANY sports events – he shut out the entire world.

Now, I have never been a sports TV kind of girl. Occasionally, I would watch a Chicago Bulls basketball game or a championship game involving the Denver Broncos. Overall, I find television sports incredibly boring. From time to time, I would sit with my husband during one of his sports TV marathons. I only did this because I missed him and wanted to be with him, not that he noticed much. Nope, his closest companion during those times was the popcorn bowl.

We had one of those popcorn poppers where you put the oil and the popcorn kernels in the bottom compartment. On the top was a reservoir for butter. As the popcorn popped, the heat from the oil would melt the butter, dripping the delicious butter over the popped corn.

In between the sports TV events, he passionately filled the popcorn bowl with its delicious buttered corn, and returned to the next sporting event. Could it get any better than this? The popping occurred over and over again throughout the marathon, until the popper was exhausted from its efforts. When he was done with it, the popper was placed in the kitchen sink, all alone, so to speak. I don't like anything left in the sink, and like a good wife, I would wash the butter-smeared popcorn popper and put it away. Good. Cleaned and out of the sink! I did this, sigh, for years.

At some point, a sense of clarity came over me, as it does for all of us, and I decided to make some changes. When this happened to me for the first time, I talked to my husband about the popcorn issue. I told him, I know you like your popcorn—a lot—but when you are finished with the popcorn popper, would you please wash it and put it away? Your mess. Not mine. Would you please clean it up? He said, "Sure".

Alas, night after night, the greasy, butter-smeared popcorn popper was still in the sink. Yes, I cleaned it and put it away. In the subsequent weeks and months, we had the discussion again and again about cleaning and putting away the popcorn popper. After each discussion, he said, "Sure. I will do that."

One night, while my husband was indulging in one of his sports marathons, I was upstairs in our bedroom watching the movie The Godfather. I had read Mario Puzo's book and enjoyed the movie. There is a scene where, at the wedding of the Godfather's daughter, a time when no Sicilian Don could refuse to see someone who seeks his counsel and help, the Godfather's nephew, Johnny Fontaine, asks for the Godfather's help to secure a part in a movie that would revive his career. The Don, after chastising his nephew for being weak, agrees to help him secure the leading role in the movie. The Godfather sends his lawyer to California to meet with the owner of Woltz International Productions. The mandate was to make the owner an offer he couldn't refuse. After a rather cold first meeting, Mr.

Woltz invites the lawyer to his home for dinner, and said he only recently learned that the lawyer worked for Vito Corleone, importantly impressive, and, showed the lawyer around his estate and stables, including an introduction to his $600,000 horse, Khartoum, whom he planned to put out for stud. Dinner later turns divisive, and Mr. Woltz said that Johnny Fontaine would never be given that movie part and told the lawyer to get the hell out of his house. The lawyer returned to New York that evening because he knew that the Godfather liked to get bad news immediately.

As the sun rose the next morning in California, Mr. Woltz awoke with a start to find his hands and silk sheets covered with blood. Thinking at first that he had been injured, he threw back the covers. At the foot of his bed was the head of his $600,000 horse, Khartoum. Several days later, Johnny Fontaine was given the starring role in the movie.

Months later for me, the butter-smeared popcorn popper continued to show up nightly in the sink. One night when my husband was in bed asleep, I went downstairs to the kitchen to get a glass of water. Seeing the popcorn popper in the sink, my mind flashed back to the horse's head scene from the Godfather. I had had enough! Stealthily, I climbed the stairs to the bedroom, cradling the greasy popper. Without awakening my husband, I carefully drew back the covers and put the popper at the end of the bed beside his feet.

An early riser, I was awake, and in the kitchen well before he awoke. When he did awake, I heard him yell, "What the hell is this?" Coming downstairs with greasy butter on his hands and feet, he said again, "What the hell is this? What?!!!" To which I replied, "This is an offer you couldn't refuse."

Marriage can be difficult at times. It requires communication and compromise. It takes work, as I have discovered. But sometimes, after endless talks and negotiation, it takes something more. It takes an offer that can't be refused.

As for me, I never had to wash the popcorn popper again.

A Shot and a Goal

I was recently watching the local news channel, as I do every morning. After the weather, local and national news, the sports overview came on. There was a clip of a national golfer who had just made some amazing hole-in-one, the shot of the century they called it. I don't remember the golfer's name. I am not a sports girl, so I didn't pay attention. What did catch my attention were the reactions of his colleagues and competitors after that hole-in-one secured his tournament win.

When I was married, all things sports were on the television, every minute of every day that we were at home. What did my husband watch?? Everything! If it was a sport, he watched it. Football, baseball, basketball, hockey, golf, soccer, wrestling, boxing, roller derby—you get the idea.

Me? Not so much. I liked basketball, but that was about it, and only certain teams. So, when all things sports were on the main TV—The Big Show, as my granddaughter calls it—I retreated to our bedroom to watch what I wanted, which was never a sporting event.

Poor Bob! On those occasions when I did indulge his sports obsession because I wanted to be with him, I was, admittedly, somewhat obnoxious. I used to find hockey announcers, of all the sports announcers, ridiculously over-the top. When a player would score a goal, they would completely lose their minds! "It's a shot and a goal!!" they would scream, as if the fate of the world had been dependent on the success of that shot.

So, regardless of the sport I was watching with him, if a player scored a touchdown, made a basket, hit a homerun, wrestled down his opponent, or hit another boxer for a knockout, I would jump up and yell, "Oh, my god, it's a shot and a goal!!!" Recognizing my sarcasm and snarkiness, I would get, understandably, the serious side-eye look, every time. His look was saying, "What are you are trying to tell me?" He knew, of course, but we didn't discuss it. It was sports, after all. I thought it was funny, but obviously, he did not.

So, back to the golfer who made the amazing shot. At the conclusion of the tournament, his colleagues and competitors swarmed him to give him congratulatory hugs. What captured my attention was a phenomenon I have noticed many times before. When guys hug each other, it appears sincere and genuine, but it almost always has to include several pats on the back. At least two and sometimes three. Why do guys do that? Women don't do that when they hug each other. Men who hug women don't do that. Why do men do that with each other?

Being the curious person that I am, I, of course, Googled that very question. What I found in numerous articles surprised me. Apparently, I am not the only one who has noticed this phenomenon.

According to one article, this open-handed pat on the back ritual has anthropological origins from when apes began to stand upright. Male apes would approach each other to determine if the other male ape was a predator or a friend. The hug was a test of this standing. The open-handed pat on the back during the hug showed the other male ape that there were no weapons in hand. A friend, not a predator.

Regardless of the anthropological history and perspective, I think the pats on the back are serious limiters. They say, "You are a great friend, or, I admire you, or well-done friend, or love you, man, but with qualification." Guys, apparently, don't generally feel comfortable getting that close to other guys. So, two or three pats on the back make a nice dismissal, a nice limiter. A boundary, I guess.

I am so glad I am a woman, for so many, many reasons, not the least of which is this. Women can hug men and other women freely, genuinely, and without limiters. No pats on the back to make it ok to be close.

Hugs, in my opinion, are among life's most amazing experiences. In my long lifetime, I have experienced nearly every variety of hug, of which there are many. But here are the varieties of hugs that stand out most in my mind.

There is the thank you, Aunt Mary, for the lovely gift hug. It is sincere, but kind of obligatory. It is a quick, arms-around-the-back, thank you for your thoughtfulness kind of hug. It is an "Oh, geez, Mom, do I have to?" kind of hug. Honestly, this hug, while usually sincere, feels best when it is over.

Next is the acquaintance—not the close friend—you haven't seen in months or years hug. It is a six-inches-between-you kind of hug that says, "So glad to see you! Let's catch up!" It is sweet and all, but often it is awkward.

The funeral hug is close, lingering, and intense. Without a word, it says I feel your pain and can't imagine what you are going through. I am here for you if you need to reach out. It is the hug that says we are all going to go through this eventually. It is a shared bond. A heartfelt bond.

There is the final we-have-shared-so-much-together, but-it-is-over hug. This is a tight, tight hug that says I have loved you so much, but we both need to move on. It is passionate; it is clingy; it is final. And, it is sad.

Hugs with your kids are among the best hugs you can ever experience. Each hug expresses so much history—from the birth to the present moment. It says, "I am so proud of you, regardless of whether the choices you are making are ones I would make or not. They are your choices, and I will support you in any way that I can". This hug says I see some of your Dad in you, and I see some of me in you. Let me guide you and keep you safe. If you have challenges, confide in me. I don't have all the answers, but I will share the wisdom I do have with you. These hugs are an affirmation of today and a positive hope for the future. These hugs are long, loving, and embrace the core of who we are as a family. I didn't experience hugs often in my childhood, but I have lavished them on my children and grandchildren. While these hugs mean so much to them, they mean everything to me.

Finally, there is the soulmate hug. Not everyone finds a soulmate, but for those of us who have, this is what it feels like. A soulmate is someone you have known long, long before you ever met them. Soulmates are exempt from gender, from zodiac compatibility, from life experiences, from sexual identity, from marital status, from economic differences, from religious differences. Soulmates, happily, are what they are. They are souls connecting without limits. Soulmates have the easy comfortability that comes with long-time history together, regardless of how long you have known each other. A soulmate makes you feel whole and happy and full of promise.

According to science, a 20 second hug with someone you care about reduces the stress hormone cortisol in the body and increases the production of oxytocin, the feel-good hormone. According to that analysis, one should hug and hug often.

That forensic analysis is well and good and informative, but this is what is so much more important. A hug from a soulmate. regardless of the duration of the hug, feels like this. Inside that hug is the safest place in the world. That hug says, for this moment, we are one. You matter to me and nothing can ever hurt either of us in this moment. It is close and intimate and warm. Feeling the other person's heartbeat against you makes you feel safe and loved and at peace.

The beauty of any hug does this. The embrace itself says all that needs to be said, regardless of the depth of emotion. A hug, well done, expresses everything without uttering a word.

Of all the hugs, pleasurable in their own way and for their own reasons, the soulmate hug, clearly, ranks at the top of the list for me. It is, truly, as the hockey announcers say, "A Shot and a Goal!"

Perspective

As you know, because I have written about it before, from as early as the age of six, I never wanted to get old. Though I had absolutely no idea of what "old" was at that age, in my child's mind, I somehow connected it to my neighborhood friends' mother. She wore baggy housedresses and wore black lace-up shoes that went up to her ankle and had chunky two-inch heels. Turtle neck shoes! They were turtleneck shoes! She wore these every day and for every occasion. Though Lois was probably only in her late thirties, in my child's mind, she became the poster child for old age. Somehow, I thought that when you got old, it was a requirement that you had to wear those chunky, black turtleneck shoes! I was so troubled by this notion that I shared my fear of this with my Dad. I told him, sobbing, that I didn't want to ever get old because I would have to wear Lois Reed shoes, and I didn't want to! Ever! He hugged me and assured me that Lois's shoes were a personal choice and that there was no requirement to wear them. He assured me that old age was a very long way off, and that I didn't need to think about that now. He comforted me, and I trusted him.

I am now at the age that is classified as "elderly". How did THAT happen? No matter. The good news is that there is no shoe requirement, and for now, I feel good and can wear any kind of shoes that I want!

My best friend and roommate was diagnosed with Alzheimer's disease two years ago, though she showed symptoms as long ago as seven years. Hard, bitter pill to swallow. But being the planner I am (when I am not in denial), we visited a number of facilities for her eventual long-term care. With my old age phobia, what I saw when we visited was through the distorted lens of fear. In wheelchairs, most residents, through my eyes, were pitiful and decrepit. After one of the visits we had, I was so troubled, I came home and threw up. What I saw, then, were my worst fears of old age, minus the shoe requirement! What kind of life could these poor people possibly have? My mother even said when she was in a nursing home, people there were just passing the days, waiting to die. How wrong she was!

D.H. Lawrence, an English writer and poet, said the degree of "otherness" from ourselves dictates the degree of fear we have from those who appear different from us. The more we seem to be different from those we see, the more frightened we become of what we don't know.

My good friend, Nancy, is now a resident in a long-term care facility near me. She can no longer walk, feed herself, or verbalize her feelings. I visit her every day. Over the course of these daily visits, something remarkable has happened. I am not sure why, though I surely think God has had an influence on this, but I have now cast aside my fear of the "otherness" that previously frightened me. Instead of viewing the residents' lives as pitiful, I have come to know them as the people they are today. Their faces and their eyes tell the stories of today's challenges, and their words tell the stories of their past experiences, loves, and the long-time wisdom they have imparted to me from their long years of living. I have learned so much from being with them!

Among the things I have learned is that a touch, a smile, and a "Hey, do you want to go for a ride" is uplifting and encouraging for both of us.

Dr. Wayne Dyer, an American self-help author and motivational speaker said when you change the way you look at something, the thing you look at changes. How right he is! I no longer look at the nursing home residents as pitiful. I have embraced them as wonderful people and friends, just as they are today, and have reveled in their lifetime stories of accomplishment and experience.

I don't know what is ahead for Nancy, or for me, for that matter. That plan is already determined. What I need to do is to trust in the plan and to have faith. Nancy no longer remembers the events or the memories we shared as friends, but she surely remembers the feelings, which she expresses every day. It is now my job to remember these memories for both of us. Instead of the sadness and anger at her rapid cognitive decline that I have felt in the past, I have learned to look at her differently. I see her as she is today and take joy in the moments, however different from the past, that we can share now together.

Events that seem tragic, burdensome, or heart-wrenching can change if we look at them differently. "When you change the way you look at something, the thing you look at changes."

The true gift is in this.

Spit

I was recently sitting on my patio, enjoying the spectacular summer sun, when I noticed a young man in his 20's come out of his condo. Now, I know a lot of people in my condo complex, but I had never seen him before. He went to his truck, took out some trash, and walked to the dumpster area to dispose of it. As he was walking back toward his condo, I thought, what a nice-looking young man! Tall and thin, his curly brown hair cascaded from slightly below his backwards baseball cap.

I tried to imagine his circumstances. Was he a recent college graduate going to pursue an advanced degree? Was he working a full-time summer job to finance his continuing education? Was he seeking a full-time professional job? It was interesting for me to run scenarios in my mind to try to figure him out. He had a very fancy black truck, so he (or someone else) obviously had means.

As he was walking back to his condo, he did something unexpected for the imaginary profile I had built in my mind for him. He lowered his head and hocked a huge loogie on the sidewalk! Yuck! Who does that? So much for the profile I created in my mind for him!! Don't mean to be stereotypical, but it caught me off guard—and yes, it was gross to me.

Then, of course, my mind went to this. Who, indeed, does that? You know me by now. I couldn't help but wonder if anyone else thought about why people spit on the street or sidewalk. So, predictably, I researched it. I am sure you are not surprised by that. Turns out, many people have been curious about this phenomenon. There are many theories, among which are these.

Some say spitting is cultural, often from emulating a father figure with a chewing tobacco habit. Apparently, it appears to represent masculinity and strength. Some say it is a form of posturing to make a male appear stronger. Some say it is a way of establishing territory, like dogs marking territory by peeing. Often, according to anecdote, men spit in the urinal or toilet before peeing. I suspect it is territorial marking. Good guess, but how would I know? To my limited knowledge, women don't do that to mark their territory or to assert their strength, nor do they need to spit in random locations. I haven't researched that with my friends or close acquaintances, though. It is way too personal to inquire about. What I am sure of is that I, personally, don't feel a need to spit before I pee; nor do I spit in random places anywhere.

To be clear, not all men spit on the sidewalk, random places, or in the urinal or toilet before they pee. There are no social or economic markers for men who spit. It is, apparently, in the end, an act to assert dominance or strength, regardless of social or economic status. From personal experience, my husband did spit before he peed. I never quite understood that, so I asked him. Habit, he would say, though I am not sure he knew why he did it any more than I did.

Ok, so why don't most women spit? Some do, I am sure. As I understand, anthropologically women have always taken a subservient role to their men. They have been the nurturers, the keepers of their homes and children. No need to posture for dominance. Their mates did that for them. Hence, no need for women to spit.

There is a categorization for some women called the Alpha female. The Alpha female has a self-confidence that is contagious. They are recognized as being impactful. They have high ambition, have high emotional intelligence, and are obsessive learners. They are strong, sought out, seek ways to help, cultivate harmony, and have exceptional confidence. And yes, with these attributes, they can comfort their Alpha males and other Alpha females alike. They are strong for everyone, with their confidence, wisdom, and compassion. No spitting for them.

I have done a self -assessment and have decided that I am, happily, an Alpha female. I am proud of that and the strength it represents. And the best part about it is, I don't have to spit anywhere to prove it! Good thing, because I have no talent for it.

Control

In the 1990's, the corporate environment was clearly a man's world. It was a time when a woman was asked if she could type, regardless of the position she applied for. Men, of course, were never asked this question, even if the position they were seeking involved some data entry and keyboarding skills. They could hunt and peck their way around the keyboard with impunity. Women were not afforded such a luxury. Not a whole lot, unfortunately, has changed in the last twenty years.

In 1991, I took a job at a company called Behavioral Interventions, or BI, Inc. I heard about the job of Monitoring Service Specialist from the mother of one of my home daycare boys. When I asked her what she did there, she told me that she made ankle bracelets. I couldn't imagine that a company called Behavioral Interventions would make jewelry. After a quick search, I discovered that the company was an electronic home arrest company that made equipment for and provided surveillance on offenders who were sentenced to electronic home arrest monitoring. Annette's job was to design and create circuit boards for the home arrest ankle bracelets that offenders wore.

Two hours after I submitted my resume to the company, I interviewed for and was offered a job as a Monitoring Service Specialist.

In the 1990's, home arrest surveillance monitoring was a fairly simple concept called presence-absence monitoring. Today, monitoring is done by GPS tracking. A person sentenced to electronic house arrest was fitted with an ankle bracelet that transmitted unique radio frequency identification information. In the offender's home was a receiver unit that looked for the unique signal emitted from the transmitter. Except for designated times when the offender was allowed to be away from the receiver, the individual on house arrest had to stay within 300 feet of the receiver unit in his home. Stray too far from the receiver or leave the house at unauthorized times would cause an alert to be sent to the Monitoring Center. Monitoring Specialists, after attempting to make contact with the offender, would then contact the supervising officer in charge of the offender.

There were four critical components to the Monitoring Specialist job– entering offender schedules allowing them to be away from their receiver units at designated times, calling offenders and officers in the event of a violation, troubleshooting equipment issues, and assisting officers with equipment installation. The two tasks that required the most finesse were having conversations with offenders about their out of -range status and assisting officers with equipment troubleshooting and installations.

Offenders would often lie about the fact that that they went too far outside their boundaries. They resented having to come to the phone, but knew they had to or risk violation of their probation or parole status. They had to be polite to the Monitoring Center staff, but often didn't want to be.

The officers were Probation and Parole officers, many of whom were Federal officers. Part of their persona was to act as if they knew everything, even if they didn't. Walking them through basic equipment troubleshooting and equipment installation was truly an art. They seldom wanted to be reminded that they may have forgotten some critical step. Using such ego saving phrases as, "I am sure you already know this, but…" helped them save face.

These skills, stereotypically, were a feminine forte, and so, not surprisingly, the majority of the Monitoring Center staff were women and the majority of offenders and officers were men. It made for an interesting dynamic.

As something of a "techie", I found the technical aspect of the job quite fascinating. While not the fastest alert processor, I was quite skilled at technical troubleshooting and equipment installation. My other skill, as a trained Counselor, was managing the fragile egos of the military men around me.

BI was what we refer to as a "cop shop". The executives, all men, of course, were criminal justice professionals and former military men. Their leadership style was authoritative, commanding, and full of bravado. While at heart basically nice people, they commanded both respect and their unique form of obedience. The corporate mantra was, "I want it right. I want it now. And I want it right now."

Six months after I was with BI, a position was created for a Monitoring Center Trainer. Increased enrollment of offenders and an expansion of the number of Monitoring Service Specialists warranted the creation of this new position. I, of course, applied. With a solid technical knowledge and a teaching background, I knew that I could build a successful program. After several interviews with key executives, I was promoted to the position. Training was of course, in their minds, a natural job for a woman.

My work was clearly cut out for me. Since no curriculum previously existed, I had to create a multi-tiered training program. There were three levels of certification and a job title change at each level. Since I had firsthand knowledge of the Monitoring Specialist job, I was acutely aware of the need for attention, precision, and accuracy. If an offender was accused of violating the conditions of his probation or parole, he could end up in court. Monitoring Center records were key in determining if someone would be sentenced to jail time or returned to prison for violations of their house arrest conditions. Such notables on our system were New York Mafia boss John Gotti and media personality Martha Stewart. For Monitoring Service Specialists, there was no room for error.

After three months of establishing the Training Certification program and training the existing staff, I was told, lightheartedly, that I trained like one of the nuns in the Catholic schools of the '70's. I was affectionately called Sister Porter and my training class was called The Obedience Center. When everyone worked hard and achieved their goals, I would reward them with multiple varieties of homemade cookies. I designed a label with a picture of a nun representing me on it and affixed it to each cookie. It said, "Sister Porter's Cookies—Make Them a Habit". This added some levity to an otherwise quite serious environment.

One of the offenders from Denver, a clearly unbalanced woman, disregarded her at-home schedule, went to a convenience store, and devised a way to place hypodermic needles in Pepsi cans. After numerous customer complaints and with the help of surveillance tapes, she was apprehended and remanded to custody.

As you can imagine, public outcry was intense. How could this happen? The woman was on house arrest. How could the public be safe from people like this? It was all over the news. Dubbed the Pepsi Lady, there was a demand for a response from BI.

An emergency meeting was called to discuss strategy and the proper response to news reporters and the public's outcry. At that meeting were seven male executives and me—a simple trainer with technical acumen. Possible approaches were discussed at length. The company could simply respond with "no comment", although that would do little to assuage the public's anger. We could "spin" the explanation, responding but not really answering the questions, a mild form of evasive lying.

I have never found lying to be to my liking. First of all, it's too much work. When you lie, you have to remember what you lied about and to whom. Secondly, the truth is always the truth and will come out eventually, regardless of the circumstances.

I learned a great deal at that meeting. After over an hour of bluster, bravado, and posturing, not one of the executives was willing to address the media or the issue at hand. It was an epiphany moment for me. These executives, I realized, had become their job titles, both inside and outside the corporation. It was how they now defined themselves, not a trait that was ever in my personal wheelhouse. They didn't want to risk scrutiny or questions about their personal performance or corporate persona.

After more conversation, I, the simple trainer, leaned in (a Sheryl Sandberg phrase), and addressed the table. "Why don't we tell the truth? There are, in fact, loopholes in today's state of the art technology that can potentially cause these events to happen. Officers and judges are aware of these limitations and still do choose to sentence offenders to electronic home arrest monitoring. I'll talk to the media."

There was a deafening silence in the room. Intuitively, I knew what they were thinking. She's a well-spoken woman, she's not an executive, and she is the perfect scapegoat. If things don't go well, we can always say she is "just a trainer". At the conclusion of the meeting, it was decided that I was to be the company spokesperson.

In the hallway after the meeting, I was approached by the Federal Program Manager. A short man with a Danny DeVito stature, he had fat sausage fingers and an annoying habit of tapping his fingertips together to make a point. "Penn," he said, (In true military style, I was referred to by my last name.) "you SHOULD take this opportunity to talk to the media. This may be your 15 minutes of fame." Not one to be intimidated by anyone and certainly not by a sausage-fingered, insecure bag of wind, I looked him straight in the eye and said, "Dave, there will be plenty of opportunities for me. I think you should do it. This may be your only chance." Clearly stunned by my gentle jibe, he smirked and walked away. He would never have talked to the media. His fragile ego had too much to risk.

The following morning, the ABC news team arrived with their camera man and a young news reporter, Ann Trujillo, who years later would become a nightly news anchor for Denver 7 News. Set up in the Monitoring Center Manager's office with a microphone attached to my blazer, the questions began. I can't tell you that I wasn't nervous. We were taping an interview that would air on the Denver News Channel's 5 and 10 o'clock news. I took a deep breath and did what I do best—I responded to the questions with authenticity and truth. I showed them how the equipment worked and told them that, in the event of a violation, we had systems in place to notify supervising officers of an offense. I didn't tell them the system was foolproof. It wasn't.

I wasn't in the building when the segment aired that night, but my daughter, a young Technical Support Specialist, was. She watched it air with the hardware and software engineers, men devoid of ego and corporate politics, men who focused on the mission, the projects, and their close teamwork. At the end of the segment, my daughter told me that, to a man, they stood up and cheered. I had become something of a hometown hero because this wasn't about me. It was about telling the truth.

Two months after the news feature, I was promoted to the position of Monitoring Center Manager. I was the only woman in an all-male executive team.

In the spring, I took a trip to Dallas to meet with Texas prison officials and Federal officers. A convicted killer, who, like the fictional character Hannibal Lecter, ate pieces of his victims, was going to be released from prison on mandatory parole and sentenced to electronic home arrest monitoring. Because Texas had an overpopulated prison system and because of the terms of his sentence, release was imminent. Texas had no choice, despite the risks we all knew were possible. Once released, the Dallas prison officials and professionals at BI knew that he would violate the conditions of his home arrest. It wasn't a question of if, but of when.

After a long meeting to discuss strategy, I flew home. Back in Boulder, I tapped the best Monitoring Specialists I could across the three 8-hour shifts. Not surprisingly to me, this specialty team was comprised of all women who were eager to show that they could accomplish this task. No one asked if they would receive extra pay for doing it and no one questioned whether it was outside the scope of their job responsibility to do so. They wanted to avoid the kind of public outcry we received at the hands of The Pepsi Lady. During this intense time, I, too, was on call 24 hours a day.

After three weeks of surveillance around the clock, he did violate his at-home schedule and was remanded back to prison to complete his original sentence, which was considerable. When it was over, we celebrated the team's dedication and diligence. Together, they prevented some unwitting Texan from becoming the snack of the week and kept BI out of the headlines. And it was done by a team of women, an accomplishment the "cop shop" culture never thought could happen. Ever. But it did.

My boss was the company COO. A former military man, he was a take charge, get it done kind of guy. You never told him you were "working on" a project. For him, something was either done or it wasn't. I truly admired him for this. His philosophy was, "I am interested in results, not excuses".

What I didn't admire was his propensity for yelling when he was displeased. If you were summoned to his office, it was like being taken to the woodshed and whipped. With the door to his office closed, if you were walking by, you could hear him yelling and pounding his fist on his desk. Both men and women were subject to his wrath and displays of anger, nor did it matter what your job title was.

Eventually, that day came for me. I was summoned to his office. So much time has passed, I don't remember the reason for his wrath. I had heard stories from other managers about their woodshed whippings long before my day came. Our Human Resource Director, a woman, of course, was completely reduced to tears by her woodshed moment.

So, I was prepared for this event. He slammed the door and yelled, "Sit down"! Not wanting to be at a level beneath him, I said," No thanks. I'll stand". As he proceeded to yell and pound his fist on his desk, I held up my index finger and said calmly, "You can disagree with me and tell me what I did wrong. You are my boss and, ultimately, I will do what you want me to do unless I find it morally unconscionable, but you will not yell at me". This was for me, clearly, a Don't Start moment. Red in the face and holding back, he made the point of his dissatisfaction abundantly clear, but he stopped yelling. Secretly, I believed then, and still do, that I gained his respect at that moment.

He never again yelled at me, although typical woodshed whippings continued for my colleagues.

Harassment in the corporate environment is a sad reality. While more women than men are harassed by virtue of their historical belief that they are powerless in the workplace, men, too, are not immune to it. I have seen at least one Marketing Director, a man so berated by his boss, that he threw up every day before he came to work.

There are multiple reasons people stay in oppressive workplace situations. They feel trapped and helpless. They feel obligations to their families. Often, they define themselves by their job titles—if I am not this, then who am I? The money, the prestige, and the presumed power can be intoxicating, enticing people to tolerate behaviors from colleagues and superiors that they otherwise never would.

The realization that we have the ultimate control over our lives comes to each of us at different times. For some, it comes early in life, for some later, and for some, unfortunately, never. We can't control the things other people say and do, but we can control our own reactions to them.

Over the years, life has presented me with challenges in the workplace and in my personal life, as it does for all of us. I have not let life's challenges define me, but rather have sought to bring my own unique definition to whatever the challenge is. Sometimes the break in the road takes us to places we never thought we would go, but to places we exactly needed to be. For every seemingly negative event that occurs, there is an upside if we look for it.

That is, after all, the ultimate control.

Backing In

Years ago, an employee who worked for me parked her car every day in a parking space that was outside of my office window. Though working on my computer most mornings, I always noticed when she arrived. From my window, I could see her drive up, move slightly beyond the open parking space, put her car in reverse, and back into the space. She was, it seemed, not at all skilled at this. It would take her three or four attempts before she could successfully back her car into the space without hitting the car on either side of her.

After months and months of watching her do this, over which time her skills did not improve, I said to her, "I have a question for you. Why do you back into your parking space? Just curious." She said, "It saves me time. I can pull out faster." Now I thought about this. That logic seemed flawed to me. If it takes four times longer to back in, where is the time saving? Where??

Since then, I have been observant of people in my condominium complex and other places who back into their parking spaces. I keep wondering why they do that and have wondered if anyone else has questioned that behavior. Turns out, I am not the only one who wonders why people back into parking spaces. There have been numerous articles written about the phenomenon of backing in. Some scientific studies have been done in the United States and other countries about the technical aspects, the psychology, and the personality types of people who back in.

The technical and safety analysis says this. Theoretically, backing into a parking space where room is limited is easier than driving straight in. Presumably, this is because when backing in, the back wheels of the car are fixed relative to the car. This means the rear wheels don't follow the same path as the front wheels, unless the front wheels are turned. When the front wheels are turned to either the left or the right depending on the direction the car is driving relative to the parking space, the car can easily be turned to back into the space. Also, technically, according to the experts, when one backs in it is safer when one exits because visibility is better, reducing the likelihood of accidents.

Ok. Let's just call that a data point. I have to say, I doubt that the average Joe or Josie, unless they are car geeks or professional truck drivers who have been taught to back in for safety, thinks about the stationary aspects of the rear wheels of a vehicle relative to the front wheels for the ease of backing in.

The psychological analysis is interesting. There have been numerous psychological analyses written about people who "back in". Some articles say that people who back in are go-getters who are more willing to do the work at the outset so they can have a smooth and easy exit, the hard work already having been done. One writer said he worked with a woman who so disliked her job that she was willing to take the time to back in so she could, as she said, "Get the hell out as fast as she could at the end of the day." Another article said that people who back in demonstrate the ability to delay gratification. They want to invest more time and effort in the now, delaying gratification, so they can enjoy the fruits of their labor later, much like the go-getter profile. One study suggests that there are people called mental rotators—those with the ability to imagine objects in other than their actual position. Those who back in tend to be mental rotators, and more men than women possess this ability. There actually is a test you can take to determine if you have mental rotation ability. I took the test. Ha! Before I even took it, I knew what the outcome would be. Frankly, at this point in my life, I would just be content to pull my car forward into my one-car garage without taking the paint off my rear quarter panel.

Ok. So, let's just call the psychological and personality analyses another data point. I am glad I did the research on this, if for no other reason than it assures me that I am not the only nut who wonders about this backing in phenomenon.

Here is what I think, based on absolutely no scientific study at all, only my own intuitive feelings about human nature. Though more men than women back in, they both seem to have the same motivation, except for the people who just want to get the hell out of places they just don't want to be. I think backing in, generally, reflects a need to validate capability and a certain superiority. It says, "Look at me. I have got this. I am so much more skilled than you are! Look how I stand out from the crowd." It is a testosterone pump, even for women who do this, to validate strength and capability. Backing in, to me, is the equivalent of spitting on the sidewalk to mark one's territory and to leave one's distinctive mark on a space. Regardless of the backing in motivation, though, I have deep respect for those who can do it.

I have always been a forward-looking kind of girl. I am usually more excited about what's ahead than I am with worrying about how to get out of it. I have always tried to mark my space, to stand out from the crowd, by being authentic and sincere, not by bragging about my potential power and superiority. This has served me well in my life.

So... I don't spit to mark my territory nor do I back into parking spaces. This is notwithstanding the fact that I haven't the slightest talent for either.

Finding Dad

Ok, so here's the deal. When you are a kid, the most important things on your mind revolve around playground fun, schoolyard adventures, and silly time spent with friends. As a young adult, career plans, finding the right soulmate, experiencing great sex, and planning for whatever future you envision for yourself is your total focus. In middle-age (whatever that is), keeping your family safe and active, and family time together is your passion. If you don't have a family and kids, the pursuit of what makes you happy—career, friends, travel—is your passionate pre-occupation.

Except for a rare few who have experienced untimely death around them, or who are TRULY neurotic planners, or who are funeral and cremation professionals, nobody knows the nuances of funerals and cremation. Who wants to know or think about that stuff? Certainly, not me.

I can't imagine why anyone would choose to go into the funeral and cremation business, unless, of course, they inherited the family business. For me, it is too up close and personal on a daily basis. But maybe people who choose this as a profession have a deeper spiritual understanding of death, and truly want to honor the dead and the feelings of their families. I am glad somebody wants to do it.

For many years, I have been trying to figure out how to get out of death. I mean, if Alexa can tell me a joke (however bad) on command, set my alarm, and play my music, surely there is a way to figure out how to get out of death. "Alexa! Cancel death for me." "Death cancelled." Be that as it may, I don't believe Alexa can do that right now, nor is there is an app for that yet. Give it time. In the meantime, I'll keep working on that for the benefit of all of us.

My 95 year-old Mother was dying. With congestive heart failure, chronic kidney failure, seizures, and having suffered a series of mini-strokes, clearly her time was going to be short. She knew this, at some level, which is why she asked me to confirm her pre-paid funeral arrangements and to check on Dad's whereabouts. What? Dad's whereabouts??

My Dad had died 24 years ago from liver cancer. A long-time alcoholic, I wasn't surprised by his diagnosis. While he was in the hospital being attended to by hospice angels, I flew from Colorado to Illinois to be with him. I spent a week, around the clock, watching him and remembering our time together when I was a young child.

Up to that point, I had very little experience with death. The most impactful, in fact, the only death I experienced, prior to Dad's death, was the death of a close high school friend who died tragically in a car accident. I remember that experience vividly. How could this happen to someone so young? What would her parents, her friends, or her dog do without her? I couldn't figure out the answers to any of those questions. For nights after her death, I couldn't sleep. I wrote a poem in tribute to her that was published in the school newspaper, and reached out to her parents as much as I could. What exactly was this death thing? It scared me.

The answers didn't come to me until I was present for my Dad's death. Mostly unresponsive during the last week

I spent with him, I tried to sum up his life as I knew it. I remembered him reading to me from the red-bound book of fairy tales. I remembered the fresh-sawn wood smell of him and his cigarette softened voice. I remembered him carrying me to my bed and kissing me softly on the cheek. I remembered the snow globe he bought me on one of his business trips. It was my mind's refuge and my place to escape during times of trouble.

And trouble there was. When I was six, my Dad wanted to move to Cincinnati where he could have had a promotion and a pay-raise as a tool salesman. My mother, hysterical often, and unsympathetic to anyone besides herself, wouldn't hear of it. She refused to leave her eight brothers and sisters, who, by all accounts, were more important to her than our family. And so, we stayed, and the constant fighting began. It wasn't until many, many years later that I learned that my Dad had other reasons for moving besides the pay raise and job promotion.

I remembered the years that he emotionally retreated from us and sought the comfort of forgetfulness in drinking. I missed him. A talented woodworker and creative artist, I so wanted to be like him. I learned much from him over the years—softness, patience, creativity, and a passion for creative arts. Even as a small child, I admired his talent and creativity. I remembered all of his beautiful creations, and I remember how humble he was about his many creative talents.

On the fifth day of his death odyssey, he, inexplicably to me, was suddenly lucid. He was alert, drinking water, taking ice chips, but not eating. What to do in the face of this rally? I had already been away from work for more than a week. Should I stay or fly back home? In the end, I decided to stay. I'm glad I did. After two days of lucidity and talking to me, he slipped back into a morphine-comforted reverie. He spent his last day frequently talking to someone. He apologized over and over again to whomever he was talking to. Whoever it was, I will never know, of course, and for what, I will never know, but apparently, it brought him the peace he needed.

I had just returned from moving the car from a two-hour parking space to the underground hospital parking garage. When I entered my Dad's hospital room, I felt something I just can't find the words to explain. There was a spiritual energy in the room that nearly took my breath away. Steadily, I approached his bed and put my hand over his heart. If I hadn't already sensed it when I entered the room, I knew it when I touched him. He was in the final, active stages of dying. I told my Mom, "Come over to the bed. Don't be afraid now. He is leaving us."

She did come over to him and was, predictably, frightened. After over 50 years together, however rocky and tumultuous, she was afraid she wouldn't know what to do without him. It was, of course, not about him, but about her. Gently, I whispered to her. "I'm going to go across the room and leave you two alone. You need to say what you need to say to him and give him permission to go in peace now."

And so, she did. When she had finished, I approached the bed again and held my Dad's hand. Within five minutes, he was gone. This was my first experience with the actual moment of death, and for me, it was beautiful and breathtaking. Did he have the fish out of water breathing? Yes. Did I hear the well documented "death rattle" in his breathing? Yes. But there was something else. There was a profound peace in the room that nearly brought me to my knees.

I am not a "religious" person. Raised Methodist, and having been actively involved in the church, I have been an intellectual believer, but not truly an emotional one. I have never clung to organized doctrines about anything, especially death and dying. But this. This was something I was totally unprepared for. When his spirit left his body, there was a peace and an overwhelming life resolution that I could never have imagined. He was at peace, and, unexpectedly, so was I. I would never look at the moment of death the same way again. I am glad for that.

Which brings me to today. Checking on Dad's whereabouts? I knew after my Dad's death, my Mom's wishes were to have their cremains mixed together in an urn and put in the grave with a headstone. I had no idea that after Dad's cremation, his ashes were put in a container (shoebox?) and housed at the Cremation Society of Illinois until my Mom's death.

Ok, so 24 years later, when I learned of this plan, I couldn't help but wonder, who does that? Why wouldn't Mom have taken his ashes, put him in a closet or another place in the house until the time of her death? Why keep him on a shelf at the Cremation Society? Maybe she didn't think she would outlive him by so many years. I just don't know. I haven't asked her that, but surely would now, if I could.

So anyway, I did what she asked. First, I went to their website to locate the phone number to call. I couldn't help but notice their landing page and the tagline they used. "Cremation Society of Illinois. Thinking Outside the Box." Really? I thought it was somewhat amusing, but wondered if other people would be offended by that. Thinking Outside the Box???? The coffin box? Sort of clever, but potentially offensive to some. Anyway, I called the Cremation Society of Illinois and talked to a professional cremation staff member. He confirmed Mom's wishes after her death, her paid-for status, and assured me of the procedures after she dies. So, I asked, "One more thing. Where is Dad? We would like his ashes shipped to my brother to keep until my Mom dies." "No problem. I will find out where he is and will call you back," he said.

A week later, I called the Cremation Society and talked to Hemio again. "Say," I said," I was just wondering if you were able to locate my Dad's cremains. Since I hadn't heard from you, I thought I would give you a call." "Hi, there, Ms. Penn. I didn't call you because I didn't have any information to give you at this point. We are still looking for his cremains. He was, apparently, at our Mt. Prospect location at one time. We had a flood there, and all the cremains were transported to other locations. He is barcoded, so we are checking all four locations to try to locate him. I will call you when we find him."

Humorously, and sadly, I kept thinking about the Elf on the Shelf. Where's Dad this week? Or next week? Where do we look to find him?

Barcoded?? Wow, I never thought about someone's remains being barcoded like grocery store items. Makes sense, I guess. I was somewhat comforted thinking that someone could take a barcode reader and locate him.

Two weeks later, I called again. As luck would have it, I talked to Hemio again. "So, hi. This is Porter Penn. Just wondering if you were able to locate my Dad's remains yet." "Well, Ms. Penn, we still haven't located him. So many cremains were moved to different locations after the flood, we are still checking all of them. I, of course, will contact you when we locate him."

Hmm. Sounded like I was getting the runaround. What would I tell Mom if she asked? What would I do if his remains were truly lost? I called my brother to tell him Dad's remains were still lost, and I was afraid they would never find him.

My brother and I have always had a close relationship and clung to each other for support during what I call the "tumultuous drinking days". One of our coping mechanisms was to adopt a sort of sick, twisted sense of humor to help keep the true pain at bay. His response to the news that they were unable to locate Dad was to say, "Did they try looking at Bob and Clara's Tavern? Maybe he stopped off for a shot and a beer." Sad, but, sickly funny.

So, being the planner that I am, I began to think about plan B. I called my daughter and talked about the situation. You have to understand my point of view, which I know isn't everyone's. I know, having been at the moment of my Dad's death, the spirit leaves the body and goes to a place of peace and forgiveness. I felt it, and I believe it. The remains are just that. Remains. So, I talked at length with my daughter about what to do if Dad's remains were truly lost. My concern was for my Mom who would be devastated if we could not find him and she knew about it.

We talked about how we could find a substitute for his ashes. My Mom could never know that his ashes were lost and unrecovered. Ever. My daughter has a high-tech smoker for everything meat. We talked about cooking chickens or beef with bones in her smoker until they were pulverized. Really—how desperate were we? Chickens or boned beef remains? Would that work? Would they look like a cremated body?

I have had more than 20 animals in my lifetime. Every one of them who died was cremated and has had their ashes secured in urns. When I moved from Fairhope, Alabama, to Windsor, Colorado, I put their urns in a box marked "Bodies". When the movers came, they asked me what was in that box. I'm not sure if they thought I cut up my neighbors and put their remains in a box or not, but I assured them it was the remains of the beloved pets I had over the years. Eventually, they were satisfied with my answer.

So, what if pulverized and cremated chickens in my daughter's smoker didn't look like authentic body remains? It was grisly, but we laughed about that. I went out to my garage where the bodies of my many long-lost animals resided. For a brief moment, I thought about the remains of my long-lost pets. What if I put them in an urn to present to my Mom? The bone fragments and ashes would look like the real deal. She wouldn't know. Ah, but alas, I would. My Mom was never a true animal lover, although she had a cat, and she fostered a group of stray cats who squatted in her backyard. Somehow, I just couldn't bring myself to mix my beloved animals in an urn to be passed off as my Dad. I just couldn't imagine them residing with her forever. At some spiritual level, I knew they wouldn't approve. And, ultimately, I wouldn't either. So, plan C was out.

On week four, I called the Cremation Society again and talked to Hemi. We were, it seemed, becoming good friends. "Hey there," I said. "Have you had any luck finding my Dad's cremains?" "I'm sorry, Ms. Penn. We really are trying to find him. I understand your concern. We have barcode readers going to each of the locations to try to find him. I really do understand your concern, and I will call you."

Mm. After all the conversations I had over the past five weeks, I was pretty certain Dad was lost.

Ok, back to the chickens. Maybe that would work. I wasn't sure how closely Mom would look at the ashes. For 95, though, she was pretty sharp. But maybe, just maybe, we could pull this off. For me, chickens would be just fine.

So, week six, I called the Cremation Society and talked to Mike, the Cremation Society Manager. Not sure why he was manning the phones, but he was. I told him I had been trying to find Dad's cremains, and I had been talking to Hemi. Apparently, he was well aware of my Dad's situation. He said, "I am so sorry. We have looked at every location, and we can't seem to find him. We'll keep looking. I will go myself to see if I can't find him. I am so sorry."

So, you know me. I took this as a teaching moment. "You know, Mike, I am not one who cares about remains. Remembering someone's life and how they touched the people around them is what matters to me. But there are clients of yours who would be devastated learning that their loved one's remains are lost. This might be a good time to review your policies and procedures in the event of a natural disaster catastrophe. Look at them carefully and make the appropriate changes to prevent this from ever happening again." "I am so sorry, Ms. Penn. I just can't say that enough."

So that is how we ended our conversation. That was it. Dad was irretrievably lost. Looks like it was to be smoked, pulverized chickens.

Less than an hour after our conversation, Mike called me back. "Ms. Penn, I have good news for you. I looked carefully at the Homewood location and found your Dad's remains. They were secured in the safe. I have them on the desk here in front of me."

I couldn't help but be skeptical. After six weeks of searching multiple locations with barcode readers, Dad suddenly shows up? I like to think that Mike wouldn't lie to me, but maybe the mini-lecture I gave him about other clients being devastated by the loss of loved one's remains made him think. What if, in desperation, he went to, for want of a better description, the lost-and-found shelf that housed the cremains of individuals who would never be claimed, and he knew it? What if he grabbed one of these and passed them off as Dad? Mm. Thinking outside the box, indeed!

Or, it actually could have been Dad. I'll never know. In the end, I didn't care and don't care. Now we had ashes to mix with Mom's, and we could get on with it. Problem solved.

I guess if there is a lesson here, it is this. When life hands you seemingly unresolvable problems, there are always chickens.

Roommates

M ost mornings lately, when I wake up with good intentions and put my feet on the floor beside my bed, Death and Grief pull back their massive fists and punch me in the stomach. I gasp for breath and the tears immediately come.

For the past several months after the death of my long-time friend and roommate, and the death of my ex-husband of 17 years, Death and Grief, the twins, have barged into my living space, uninvited. The vulnerable part of me tells me to invite them in so that we can have our unpleasant daily and nightly chats. The angry, wounded, and confused part of me wants to slam the door, lock it, and put my back up against it to keep them out. I don't want to talk to them; I don't want them in here, and I don't want to acknowledge their existence. Apparently, it doesn't matter what I want. Locked doors can't keep them out. I know this. They just push harder and make their way in anyway.

Every time they talk to me, which is multiple times during the day and night, they deliver the same message. "The father of your children and your best friend in the world have died within months of each other. They are gone, the other important parts of your life have changed, and there is nothing you can do about it. You are, it seems, alone. That is why we are here—to remind you of that and to give you the only company that you have now, or ever will have." Each time, their message brings me to my knees.

To make matters worse, the twins have invited their friend, New Life, to join them. Of the three, New Life frightens me the most. He has a nebulous form and no face. Try as I may to sketch out his form and his face in my mind, I fail. He remains formless and faceless.

Since I know I can't keep the three of them out of my living space, lately I have tried ignoring them. I refuse to talk to them and occupy my time completing mindless to-do lists. I do laundry, clean the house, go to the bank, wash the car and fill it up with gas. Dumb stuff, I call it. Tasks that need to be done but are devoid of emotion.

I can tell that Death, Grief, and New Life don't like it much when I do this. They stare at me and stand way too close. I feel the hot breath of their reality on my neck. It is at these times that I pace back and forth, hyperventilating, in hopes of forcing them to go away. I quickly learn, much to my dismay, that now that they have arrived, they are never going away.

On one of those days, as the three of them sit on my sofa, satisfied by all of the sadness, despair, and fear that I have fed them, I sneak off into my office and close the door. This is my quiet place where I can shift into my cerebral and analytical mind.

You have a problem, I tell myself. You now have three Roommates who are not going away. You don't like them, but they are here. They have loomed large over you since their arrival, mostly because you have indulged them. So, what are your choices? You can throw a party for them every day, inviting them to torture you with sadness and fear. They would love that! It would give them the strength and power that they want. Or you can do something else.

One of your friends, no stranger to grief and sadness, said sometimes working the to-do list is just what is needed for a while. Not what we want, but a small step in moving forward. What you want will come later. One day at a time. It will be ok. After this sage and heartfelt advice, you did what you always have done. You parked this advice in a corner of your mind, determined to get to that positive place by taking your own route to get there.

You know, you do, that you are going to have to have "the talk" with the three of them. No more ignoring them with rote to-do lists. No more indulging them. But what do you say and how?

As I am sitting at my computer desk this day, my eye catches a framed letter that my daughter wrote me on my 60th birthday. While I have seen it every day for years in my office, it has been a long time since I have actually read it. As I am reading it, I focus on this paragraph. "Over the past 60 years, you have been a teacher, a mother, a leader. You have counseled many and helped shape and give guidance, not only to myself, but to children, friends, and co-workers. You have been many things to many people, and in the future, I hope you find out what you need to be for yourself."

Her words resonate for the first time in more than a decade. As I sit and think about them, they are profound. What do I need to be for myself? After this reflective time alone, I think I know. I need to cherish past memories, never let them go, but never let fear and sadness keep me from moving forward. I have much to give, and I won't let these uninvited Roommates keep me from doing just that. I can best honor those that I have lost by moving ahead and staying positive. Ah, I think I now know what to say to these unwanted Roommates

Days later, I know it is finally time to have "the talk". I am ready. As the three of them sit on my sofa, staring at me, I summon my courage, and standing in front of them, say what I need to say.

"You three have occupied my home and my life for six months. I didn't invite you in, as many households don't, but you invited yourselves. Death and Grief, you are the most vocal and hurtful. New Life, while passive, you are the most frightening. For months, you three have overtaken my feelings and my actions. While I know I can't get rid of you, I know this. As of today, you are no longer running this show. I am. Death and Grief, I will no longer let you occupy my mind every minute of every day, and you will no longer greet me in the morning with a punch in the gut. New Life, I know all about you. You are here because of the other two and not by your choice."

"Today, I am going out because I want to and need to. New Life is going with me. We are going out every day and some nights until New Life has a face and a form. I know New Life will eventually become my friend and will share my life in making new memories and new traditions. I am so looking forward to our adventures and to our friendship. Death and Grief, you are staying here. When we return, we will acknowledge you, but you will no longer control us. That is the way this show is going to run now!

Oh, and by the way, in the spirit of hospitality, and since I will no longer feed you with my sadness and despair, feel free to help yourselves to anything in the fridge."

That Dog Don't Hunt

I was just sitting here in my desk chair, with my feet propped up on my bed. This is my place to think about events in my life that have been so important to me.

As I take a renewed View from the Drain, I remember so many events and encounters that have brought me happiness and hope. I am so glad that I can remember them all. We all have those moments, the promise of which has made us joyous and optimistic every day that we have experienced them. Ah, the everyday anticipation of what is to come gives us that all important hope and rush of life! That, of course, is the same for all of us, regardless of the specifics.

Sometimes, it is the unbridled possibility of a new, desired job. Sometimes, it is the thrill of a new courtship that results in a long-term relationship. Sometimes, it is the promise of the children not yet born. Sometimes, it is the excitement of a move to a place where we can begin our lives over again. Sometimes, it is the security of a deep, meaningful friendship. These feelings and events are the pinnacle of what life has to offer. They are to be savored and embraced, regardless of the eventual outcome.

A man (or a woman), who has a hunting passion, buys an expensive hunting dog to enhance the excitement of the hunt. They place their trust and their hope that the dog would do what it was bred to do. Ahh, the possibilities are limitless! How exciting! A new dimension to a long-time passion has begun!

After purchase, the owner excitedly takes the dog out to the field to watch it perform during the hunt. The excitement and anticipation takes the owner's breath away! It doesn't get any better than this!

Hmm… The dog runs and sniffs and has no interest in the hunt, only in its outdoor freedom. The owner thinks, well, since the dog was bred for this, with a little training, it will perform as expected.

After months and months and months of training and effort, it is clear, that dog don't hunt.

Sometimes, our deep hopes and expectations don't turn out to be what we wanted them to be. The excitement and anticipation were *so* there, but the eventuality was not.

What to do? This is a question for each of us. The owner could shoot the dog because it didn't live up to the expectations and perceived promise. Or, the owner could no longer choose to hunt with the dog and could love it for what it does have to offer—companionship and love, without the original hunting expectation.

This choice comes to all of us during our lifetime journey.

I know what my choice would be.